Prayer

For Catherine

who taught us all how to pray

Prayer

Amy Welborn

Our Sunday Visitor Publishing Division
Our Sunday Visitor, Inc.
Huntington, Indiana 46750

Nihil Obstat
Rev. Michael Heintz
Censor Librorum

Imprimatur
✠ John M. D'Arcy
Bishop of Fort Wayne-South Bend
June 27, 2002

The Nihil Obstat and Imprimatur are official declarations that a book or pamphlet is free of doctrinal or moral error. No implication is contained therein that those who have granted the Nihil Obstat or Imprimatur agree with the contents, opinions, or statements expressed.

The Scripture citations used in this work are taken from the New American Bible with Revised New Testament and Psalms, copyright © 1991, 1986, 1970 by the Confraternity of Christian Doctrine, Inc., Washington, D.C. Used with permission. All rights reserved. No part of the New American Bible may be reproduced by any means without permission in writing from the copyright owner. Excerpts from the English translation of the Catechism of the Catholic Church, Second Edition, for use in the United States of America, copyright © 1994 and 1997, United States Catholic Conference – Libreria Editrice Vaticana. Used with permission. The author and publisher are grateful to those publishers and others whose materials, whether in the public domain or protected by copyright laws, have been used in one form or another in this volume. Every reasonable effort has been made to determine copyright holders of excerpted materials and to secure permissions as needed. If any copyrighted materials have been inadvertently used in this work without proper credit being given in one form or another, please notify Our Sunday Visitor in writing so that future printings of this work may be corrected accordingly.

Copyright © 2002 by Our Sunday Visitor Publishing Division,
Our Sunday Visitor, Inc.

All rights reserved. With the exception of short excerpts for critical reviews, no part of this book may be reproduced in any manner whatsoever without permission in writing from the publisher. Write:
Our Sunday Visitor Publishing Division
Our Sunday Visitor, Inc.
200 Noll Plaza
Huntington, IN 46750

ISBN: 978-0-87973-544-9 (Inventory No. 544)
LCCN: 2002107146

Cover design by Tyler Ottinger
Cover photo by John Zierten
Interior design by Sherri L. Hoffman
Interior illustrations by James Douglas Adams

PRINTED IN THE UNITED STATES OF AMERICA

Contents

Introduction

WHERE WOULD YOU BE without your friends?

Imagine life without them. Pretty wretched thought, isn't it?

No one to vent to about your parents. No one to help you put life in perspective. No more incredibly intricate inside jokes. No one to confide in about your hopes and dreams of becoming a professional surfer/pediatrician. No one to help you edit your English paper. No one to write your English paper. Just kidding about that last one.

Friends are really a gift from God, and you know it.

> A faithful friend is a sturdy shelter;
> he who finds one finds a treasure.
> A faithful friend is beyond price,
> no sum can balance his worth.
> — Sirach 6:14-15

How did your friendships start? How did they develop? What's the most important thing you do to keep those friendships going?

Would communication have anything to do with it?

Endless telephone conversations. Secrets. Confidences. Laughter. Tears. E-mail and instant messaging. Jokes. Notes in class. Eyes rolling in despair as your geometry teacher plods through yet one more proof. And hugs. Can't forget hugs.

Now, try to imagine a reverse situation. Imagine there's a person running around school proclaiming his deep and abiding friendship with you to everyone he sees. The problem is, you barely know the guy.

Sure, you gave him change for a dollar once in front of the soda machine, and he suffers through biology class with you, and no way he's your enemy, but friends? Hardly. How can you be friends with someone you never talk to?

Oh.

Boy, you are good. You've connected the dots all by yourself, without any help from me.

How can we be friends with God if we never communicate with Him?

Now, LET'S GET ONE really important thing straight before we go on.

God is friends with us no matter what.

More than friends, in fact. God loves us deeply and yes, even passionately.

How do you know this?

Because He made you, that's why.

If you really believe that God created you, you can't avoid the conclusion that He loves you. After all, God doesn't make things by accident. Everything He does is completely, totally on purpose. And that includes you.

So, next time you're lying in your room, feeling a bit sorry for yourself and singing the "nobody understands me" song, remember that:

I'm here. That means I'm loved.

So when it comes to friendship, the problem is not on God's side. From His point of view, there's no problem. He's our best friend, most intimate and faithful lover, and most passionate and protective parent, all rolled into One. The One.

But, as the old saying goes, it takes two to tango. And how in the world can God dance with you when you're just hiding in the bathroom, obsessing over your hair in the mirror?

In other words, if you're not feeling close to God right now, if God is distant and totally mysterious and religion is quickly becoming just a bunch of words and abstract ideas instead of something personal and powerful, did you ever stop to think about the reason why?

When was the last time you prayed, anyway?

OH, COME ON BACK. I didn't mean to get you all huffy. I know — you have been praying. You've been saying your prayers every night before you go to sleep ever since you could talk. You go to Mass. You say grace.

But still . . .

Things aren't like they were when you were younger, are they?

Just like your friendships, prayer was really simple when you were little. When you played with your friends, it was all very uncomplicated. You got together, you shared, you had fun. Prayer was pretty much the same way: You never had a hard time trusting that your sim-

ple words were shooting straight up to God's ears and that He was listening.

But now, years later, everything is just a bit more complicated. In every part of life, it seems.

Friendships are more complicated, and maybe even harder to maintain. You're discovering that people are pretty profound creatures and not always easy to understand. You could, of course, continue conducting friendships on a totally superficial level, but while that might be fun, it doesn't satisfy for long. It takes time and, more importantly, an emotional investment to build good friendships.

A friendship with God is exactly the same way. It's not that our words need to get fancier or our prayers longer and more intricate just because we're older. Not at all — every prayer Jesus prays in the Scriptures is a model of simplicity, as a matter of fact. No, it's our hearts that need to expand.

In other words, to have a healthy and powerful friendship with God, you need to share with Him the greater depths and complexities you're discovering in yourself every day.

No more coasting. Put that skateboard away.

That's not easy, for a lot of reasons: We're afraid. Other things seem more important than God. In fact, if things are going well in most areas of our lives, we may not even really feel the need to deepen our friendship with God.

But do you know what?

God's still there.

Ready with love, ready with grace, ready with healing, ready with answers, ready with nothing less than wholeness and utter peace.

> Look at Him who is looking at you.
> — St. Thérèse of Lisieux

If you think life is good now, just imagine what it would be like if God, the source of all love, all peace and all joy, was a more intimate

part of it. Just try to imagine the vivid hues life might take on if you were walking around looking at it not just through your own eyes, but through the filter of what God has to say about it all: His very own creation.

Are you listening?

No matter how you answered that question up there, this book is for you.

If you answered "no," then I hope you'll find a reason or two to go ahead and start listening to God's voice in your heart.

Even if you answered "yes," I would bet good money that there's another word fighting to come out after that affirmative: " . . . but."

But I'm not sure whether it's God I'm hearing or those are just my own thoughts.

But I really want to pray at a deeper level.

But I'm just a little scared to put my whole self into this prayer thing — who knows what will happen if I do?

I hope this book will help you answer your questions, too.

There's one thing you have to remember, though. Reading about prayer and expecting your life to magically change and your spirit to suddenly soar to the heights of heaven is about as realistic as think-ing dinner's going to appear on the table just from reading a cook-book.

You've got to do it. You just have to — pray, that is.

You have to scrape out a little time — just a little — maybe ten minutes a day — to be absolutely by yourself, away from people, away from noise (turn off that stereo, I'm telling you!), to be alone with God and put what you're learning into practice. You also will most def-initely need a Bible, so if you don't have one, go back to the store where you bought this little masterpiece and spend a little more money.

And if you're tempted to say "no, not now" to this adventure of deepening your relationship with God through prayer, take a minute

before you run off to do all of those much more important things, and ask why.

Why don't I want to pray more?

Once you have your answer, imagine saying it. Not just to anyone, though. Open up your imagination and in that fertile field, picture yourself explaining why you don't want to be closer to God, to...

... the One who's waiting for you like a father waiting for His prodigal child.

... the One who's searching you out like a lost sheep every single time you wander away.

... the One who has said "Go, your sins are forgiven" more times than you can count.

... the One who formed you in your mother's womb.

... the One who died, nailed to cross.

I thought so.

See, there is absolutely nothing to fear from prayer or the God you're going to meet in that prayer place. He loves you. Forever. No matter what.

And He's waiting.

Let's go.

> Mental prayer in my opinion is nothing else than an intimate sharing between friends; it means taking time frequently to be alone with Him who we know loves us.
>
> — St. Teresa of Ávila, *Life*

I Don't Need to
Pray Because . . .

CHAPTER 1

I Don't Need to Pray Because...

...God's In My Heart All the Time

WELL, SURE.

God is with you constantly, and has been since the moment you were a darling little itty-bitty embryo.

> *You formed my inmost being;*
> *you knit me in my mother's womb.* (PSALM 139:13)

And God's with you right now, as you're reading this book. He's with you at school. He's with you on the practice field. He's with you in the bathroom (eeeew... but true!). He's with you while you scarf down your nourishing breakfast of cola and corn chips. (You think I'm kidding? I taught high school. I've seen it.)

God — is — with — you — every — second.

> LORD, *you have probed me, you know me:*
> *you know when I sit and stand.* (PSALM 139:1)

Got it. Now answer a question for me. So what?

Why does God's gracious presence with you somehow imply that you don't have to do anything in response?

Imagine, for a moment, that you're with your family at dinner. It's one of Mom's typically fabulous meals. (And you do tell her it's fabulous, at least every once in a while don't you? She needs to hear it, and

believe me, complimenting a meal racks up a whole lot of points that just might come in handy someday.)

Anyway, dinner is great, everyone's there together, chattering away, until a moment comes when, deep in your Tuna Tortilla Surprise, you notice silence has suddenly descended. You raise your eyes. You see everyone at the table, from Grandpa to the baby, staring at you. Waiting. For what?

"Well?" Dad asks. "What do you think?"

Of what? What do I think of what? You can't help but wonder.

For you see, while you were certainly physically present in this room full of very real, very lively, very loud people, somehow, you hadn't heard a word anyone was saying.

You were way too deep in meditation — about what, we won't ask, because we really don't want to know.

But the fact is, your physical presence didn't guarantee — well, presence.

I Don't Need to Pray Because . . .

You were there, but you weren't there. You weren't listening, you weren't relating to anyone, and you couldn't tell us what color Grandpa's tie was if we offered you a million dollars. (It was green with violet polka-dots, by the way. Retro, but nice.)

So there's lesson No. 1: Presence doesn't automatically mean relationship.

Now with God, of course, the problem is all on our side. God's never inattentive, His focus never wanders, He never turns His back, not even for a second:

> *Even all the hairs on your head are counted.*
> (MATTHEW 10:30)

But when it comes to us — well, we might like to talk big, like we're some sort of deep mystics, constantly in touch with God, but let's be honest.

That's not exactly the case, is it?

After all, if it were true that we were incredibly aware of God all the time, our lives might be just a little bit different — in a word, we'd be saints. But we're not. We live in a way that's more like what a mystic named Meister Eckhart described centuries ago:

> God is near to us, but we are far from him. God is within;
> we are without. God is at home; we are abroad.
> — SERMONS 6, *THE KINGDOM OF GOD IS AT HAND*

So it's a great, comforting truth that God is present with us all the time. But unless we consciously try to plug into that presence, we're like we were at dinner that time: sitting there kind of pathetically, in our own private space, wondering what everyone else is talking about, alone even though we're in a room full of people.

Think of it this way. It would be very nice for a dear friend to stand in front of you telling you how much he liked you. But what impact would that have on your life if you met his presence and his affection with nothing but the most cursory acknowledgment, day after day,

never responding, never sharing, never even looking him in the eye? How would your friendship grow? Would you even have a friendship?

That's exactly the way it is with us and God. God's always present to us in love, but we must make a conscious effort to be present to Him, too, or else we don't really have a relationship with Him.

That's what prayer is.

Sure, there are lots of ways to do this thing called prayer: We do it with spoken words, we do it with songs or even silently. We do it alone, we do it with others. We use other people's words, or we make up our own. We use the Bible to help us, or we use a sunset. We come to God in joy and praise. We come to thank Him and to beg Him for mercy. We turn to Him to ask for help for ourselves and others. We come to Him to find truth and meaning, and in the end, we're coming to Him to find ourselves. Our true selves — way down underneath the worries and needs, underneath the person everyone on earth from our parents to friends to advertisers tells us that we should be. We know there is a true self, made for joy and peace. The only other One who knows this true self is the One who made it , and that's God. The journey to that true self, the self we long for, isn't that long really. It's just as long as the journey to God, and you know how far that is, right?

Any way you choose to do it, when you're opening your heart, turning to God, talking to Him, listening and searching, what you're doing at that moment is acknowledging God's presence and responding to it.

That, in a nutshell, is prayer.

Here it is in another, slightly bigger and more brilliant nutshell, fashioned by a great pray-er, St. Thérèse of Lisieux:

> For me, prayer is a surge of the heart; it is a simple look turned toward heaven, it is a cry of recognition and of love, embracing both trial and joy.
>
> — MANUSCRITS AUTOBIOGRAPHIQUES, C 25R

 I Don't Need to Pray Because . . .

So for all of our rather arrogant claims that sure, we can have a great relationship with God without actually ever, well, taking time to develop a relationship, there's really only one thing to say, and the person who said it is another great pray-er, St. Teresa of Ávila:

> We are always in the presence of God, yet it seems to me that those who pray are in His presence in a very different sense.

If you've ever known anyone who is authentically, truly prayerful, you'll know what St. Teresa was talking about. There's a peace and tranquility, a real goodness that shines through a person who's really aware of God's presence.

When you think about it, you just have to ask: Why wouldn't everyone, given the choice (which we are) want to live that way?

You also have to ask yourself: Given the choice (which you are), why wouldn't *you* want to live that way?

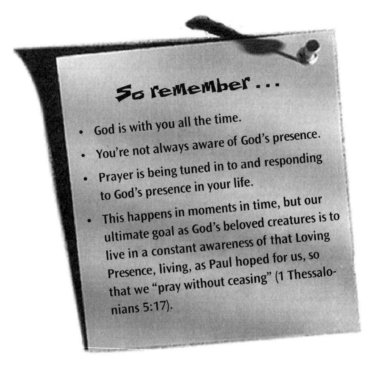

So remember . . .

- God is with you all the time.
- You're not always aware of God's presence.
- Prayer is being tuned in to and responding to God's presence in your life.
- This happens in moments in time, but our ultimate goal as God's beloved creatures is to live in a constant awareness of that Loving Presence, living, as Paul hoped for us, so that we "pray without ceasing" (1 Thessalonians 5:17).

CHAPTER 2

I Don't Need to Pray Because...

...God Already Knows Everything I Feel: I Don't Have to Tell Him

DO YOU LOVE your dad? Mom?

I hope so. Sure, you get irritated with each other on occasion, and have daily (hourly?) disagreements on everything from the exact definition of "clean the kitchen" to your whole entire future, but there's no doubt you love them, they love you, and everyone is totally aware that everyone loves each other. Got it?

So, since we're all clued in to our deep mutual affection, I guess that means we don't have to show it. No hugs, no cards, and no gifts. And, of course, no words.

No? Well, why not? After all, we understand that we love our parents and our friends. We don't actually ever have to express it, do we?

Well, maybe. Maybe such a household, stripped of all expressions of affection, sounds pretty dismal. After a few weeks of this, in fact, we might just start doubting whether the feelings exist at all, it's been so long since we've heard them expressed.

Now, you're smart, so you've already seen the limitations of this analogy. God, you're quite correctly pointing out, isn't a human being. He's omniscient — which means He knows everything, which would also seem to mean that He doesn't need our tinny little voices informing Him that we love Him. He doesn't need reassurance. Even Paul said as much to the pagan Greeks in Athens:

> *... nor is he [God] served by human hands because he needs anything. Rather it is he who gives to everyone life and breath and everything.* (ACTS 17:25)

And if you said all this, you'd be right. About God.

But would you be right about us?

Consider this honestly. If we really love someone, whether it's another human being or God, we have a very, very hard time keeping it inside.

Maybe you know this is true because you have had the great fortune of hanging around someone who's just fallen in love. She's caught up in the romance of the ages, an eternal flame that will never, ever, ever die out.

And she won't ever, ever shut up about it, either.

Oh, that's not quite right. She will stop talking about it from time to time — during those moments she's talking to the amazingly perfect object of her affection.

But even short of this rather extreme example, common sense tells you that authentic love is always expressed. It's expressed in different

 I Don't Need to Pray Because ...

ways for different people in all the varied types of friendly and romantic relationships, but no matter what, if love is there, it is expressed in word and deed.

And if it wasn't, we'd be sorely tempted to wonder whether there was really any love there at all.

Maybe — just maybe — the same holds in our relationship with God, which is, in another simpler word, our faith.

When we love God, we can't help but express it. When we stop and realize exactly who God is, the next natural step — after we catch our breath — is praise. I mean, what other response can there be to the One who is Being, Truth, and Life? Rejection? Criticism? Nitpicking? Gee, you're hard to please. As for the rest of us, we just have to bless. We have to sing. We have to praise.

That's where all the rest of prayer starts — with praise. There are lots of other kinds and styles of prayer, all of which we'll be discussing in this book, but each and every one of them begins with the same attitude:

Praise.

> Come, let us sing joyfully to the LORD;
> cry out to the rock of our salvation.
> Let us greet him with a song of praise,
> joyfully sing out our psalms.
>
> — Psalm 95

Songs of praise, words of praise, thoughts of praise. Love letters, notes, and songs to God. All murmured, sung, and shouted and even just breathed, not because of anything God has done, but — and here's a slightly tricky part of praise — because of who God is.

At first, this might seem odd. It's not exactly what we're used to. We're accustomed to adding reasons to our praise, most of them related, quite frankly, to good stuff that's happened to us. We praise God because we got well. We praise God because He had the superb taste to create us. We praise God because we're currently leading such a fabulous life.

This may seem harmless enough, but let's jump back to our relationship analogy to see if it really is.

Would it warm your heart to have a dear friend walk up to you and announce, "I really care for you because you lent me twenty bucks last week."

Would you be reassured of your dad's love if he told you at dinner, "You know, kid, I really love you because you had such a great report card yesterday."

Or — getting back to that Big Romance — what if Ms. Love of Your Life whispered that you were the one for her because . . . you gave her a great Christmas gift.

Not exactly what you were looking for, was it?

No. You were probably hoping that if anyone bothered to tell you how much they cared for you it wouldn't be for any of your accomplishments, but for something just a bit more basic: who you are.

You were hoping for that, not only because it gives you a greater sense of security in case your next report card isn't so great or all you could afford next Christmas was a box of candy canes, but because you know that the only stance worthy of the name "love" is caring for someone for who they are, not for what they do.

So flip it around once more. If praise is our love letter to God, then our praise should be rooted in that same attitude: love for God simply because God is God.

Now, the other stuff — the stuff that God does for us — will come into this, in another form of prayer: thanksgiving. But even that's trickier than it sounds, because what all of the Big Cheese Pray-ers tell us, over and over again, is that our thanksgiving prayers aren't just for the things we like, but even for the things we don't.

Yikes.

But more on that later. Right now, let's stick with praise.

I Don't Need to Pray Because . . .

Can you do it?

Sure you can. Maybe you can't sit there for thirty minutes in constant, intense praise, but you can close your eyes for a minute, remember who God Is, and breathe a little "Alleluia."

And if you do this, the strangest thing might happen.

In offering praise to God for who He Is, the eyes of your soul will open just a bit to take in the beauty, not just of God, but of all God has made.

In taking time in the middle of the day (or night) to remember God and just be present to Him for no reason except love, you just might find yourself filled with a little bit more love than you had a minute ago, with just a little clearer vision. You can do this anywhere: in class, while you're waiting for the teacher to get himself together for another fun session with quadratic equations; in line at the store; stopping at a traffic light; or even during six spare seconds at your locker. You can close your eyes and be mindful of who God Is and how much He loves you.

???

STOP ME IF I'M WRONG, but I do believe you're growing.

Why? Because you're letting God in, not because you want something, but just because God is. And because you belong to God, you're finding that your spirit, just a little more open and aware today than it was yesterday, fits rather snugly into the arms He's holding out in love.

> In prayer, we open ourselves out to God, and
> this process is one of liberation and awakening.
> — Kenneth Leech, *True Prayer*

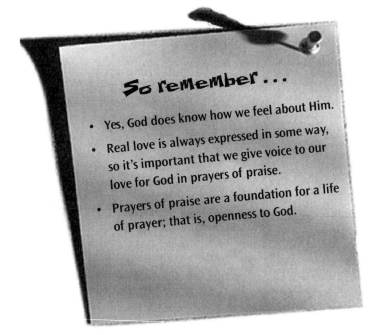

So remember . . .

- Yes, God does know how we feel about Him.
- Real love is always expressed in some way, so it's important that we give voice to our love for God in prayers of praise.
- Prayers of praise are a foundation for a life of prayer; that is, openness to God.

 **I Don't Need to Pray Because . . .**

CHAPTER 3

... God's In Control: My Prayer Doesn't Influence Him

YOU THOUGHT you asked politely.

Actually, you made a quite conscious effort to be astonishingly, incredibly polite. You'd even made sure to behave flawlessly for about a week before you posed the question.

But after all that, they still said no.

It's true. Despite your best intentions, your parents still said no to that post-prom weekend at the lake with fifty of your closest friends. You didn't even have the chance to share the news that the gathering would be unchaperoned before they answered, without even looking up from the newspaper.

This is not the first time it's happened, either. Lots of people have said no to you in the past: your teachers, when you asked for an extension for your paper on the "Philosophical Assumptions of Burger King Commercials"; your youth minister, when you wanted to play a fifteen-minute cut from 2Kewl4U's latest album as an opening prayer; and your parents, when ... well, we don't have enough time for that.

It's enough to discourage anyone. But is it enough to convince you that because the answer to your questions is sometimes "no," that your questions weren't, therefore, answered at all? Or that your parents weren't listening? Or that you are, in the end, totally powerless and unable to influence them at all?

No, you probably wouldn't think any of that. After all, you've heard "yes" to your requests a lot more than you've heard "no," so you're fully aware that you are listened to and your requests are, indeed, heard.

Some people — maybe you, maybe not — think of the possibility of God answering prayers in just that way, though. Because they don't get the answer they want to prayer, or don't seem to hear an answer at all, they conclude that either God doesn't exist, or that if He does exist, He doesn't answer prayers.

In other words, He doesn't give a hoot about you or your needs.

Is any of that true? Or is this just one more case of us not really understanding what prayer is all about, and blaming God for what is really, kind of, sort of, actually our fault? Again?

The first thing we really have to do, though, is figure out why we're praying for things to happen at all.

This is something you may have wondered about from time to time yourself. Say Grandpa's sick. We're praying for healing everywhere we go: at home, at Mass, and at school. Well, how exactly do we expect this to help? What good will it do to pray that Grandpa be

healed? If God wants him healed, wouldn't He do it without us suggesting it? Does asking God to heal Grandpa imply that He either isn't aware that he's sick or would withhold His intentions to heal until the right people asked in the right way? In short, does God really need our input into the running of the universe?

The brief answer is that He may not need it, but He must certainly want it. How do we know this? Two ways. First, Jesus told us He does.

When you're grappling with faith matters, it's really important to always look first to Christ. He wasn't, after all, simply another wise teacher among many that the world has produced. He's God, right? He rose from the dead, right? Consider this carefully, and force your mind to stick with it: If Jesus is God, everything He said is true and right. So what did Jesus have to say about prayer, anyway?

> *And I tell you, ask and you will receive; seek and you will find; knock and the door will be opened to you.*
> *For everyone who asks, receives; and the one who seeks, finds; and to the one who knocks, the door will be opened.* (LUKE 11:9-10)

Jesus clearly lets us know that God wants our lives to be led in constant communion with Him, depending on Him for every need.

> *He would not urge us to ask, unless He were willing to give.*
>
> — St. Augustine

Secondly, when you look at history and nature for the ways of God, it seems pretty clear that He's set the whole thing up to be a joint venture between Him and us.

The exact balance between God and human action within creation is something we'll never know. It's been a source of mystery and discussion ever since people started thinking about God. But don't let that mystery frustrate you too much. After all, what we're talking about here is essentially the problem of cause and effect, and, truth be told, that's never as easily determined as we think it is, even looking at it from a purely human standpoint.

Think about how certain events in your life came to be. Why do you live where you do? Why do you play softball and not soccer? Why do you love the theater? Why do certain things make you angry and other things fill you with peace? Why, in fact, do you exist at all?

No, there's no simple answer to any of those questions. The shape of our lives is the result of countless factors, woven from a variety of human choices, desires, emotions, accidents, and God's grace.

So if we can't easily tease apart the cause of the human and natural effects we live with, we really can't expect to be able to make two neat lists of "Our part" and "God's part" of events.

But for us, as Christians, this is what we do believe, even if we can't effortlessly separate God's part from our part:

God created the world, and God is involved with the world. He influences what happens.

God created human beings with free will, intelligence, and love. We're involved with the world, too. We influence it, too.

I Don't Need to Pray Because ...

And how do we know this? The same way we know a lot of things about our faith: through what's been revealed to us.

Think back through the Bible. Think of Abraham, Moses, and King David. Think of Mary, Jesus, the apostles, and Paul. Consider the stories we tell about them — every one of them is a mix of human and divine action. Sometimes God enters the picture first — sending an angel with strange news to Mary, knocking Paul off his horse. But sometimes we seem to take the initiative: people asking Jesus for healing, or Abraham arguing with God about the destruction of Sodom

God acts and we act. It's important to remember that God's action is in no way dependent on us, except in one respect:

Because God created us as creatures with free will, He can't, in justice to what He's made, violate that freedom. He can startle and shock us, and stand in front of us in ways that are mighty hard to ignore (back to Paul and that horse on the road to Damascus again), but the fact is, we can still ignore him. Paul could have kept persecuting Christians. Sure, he might not have been able to see them, but he could have continued persecuting them. Mary could have said no to Gabriel. The apostles could have declined Jesus' invitation to follow them.

What's clear from the Scriptures is this: **God is not distant, and we are not powerless**. We don't know why, and sometimes the results may lead us to wonder whether God really knew what He was doing, but the fact is, this is the way it is.

Maybe a good way to see this is to think about Jesus and miracles.

Jesus' miracles are always and everywhere tied up with faith. Think about how many times Jesus says to someone He's about to heal: "Your faith has saved you." And think about this strange little passage from the Gospel of Mark:

> So he was not able to perform any mighty deed there [in
> his hometown of Nazareth], apart from curing a few sick

*people by laying his hands on them. He was amazed at
their lack of faith.* (MARK 6:5-6)

There's really no clearer picture of the complicated, mysterious relationship between our attitude and God's actions. God is absolutely free. But He is also love, and God's love involves something very important: loving His human children for what they are — free.

So there's the strange reality we must live with: God, utterly free, chooses to work with us in shaping creation.

Now, you could spend a lot of time arguing with this. Some people do. "God could have done things differently," they say. Sure.

But so what?

Yes, indeed, God could have decided to create new human beings from dirt every time. But He didn't. He chose to involve human beings in the process through our amazing, miraculous gift of sexuality.

I suppose that when God wanted to introduce the Good News of salvation into the world, He could have sent each person on earth an individual angel with an intricate explanation of how the whole business works and an explicit set of instructions carved on a personal rock. But He didn't. He sent Christ, who then sent weak, flawed, sinful human beings out to tell the rest of us. Strange, but true. Inefficient in our eyes, perhaps, but seriously, given who God is, and given who we are (free, remember), what else could He do?

God gives us the skills and the imagination to work with Him, and because we're creatures of both body and spirit, we can work with Him in both body and spirit. We can love, talk, help, bring comfort and healing, all with our hands and ears and the rest of our bodies, and we can use our spirits. We can pray.

There are two dimensions to this type of prayer that involves us in God's work. The first is called prayer of petition, and it is mainly about ourselves, the pray-er. In prayers of petition, we look to God for our own needs. As you can probably figure out, the prayer of petition

I Don't Need to Pray Because . . .

starts from an awareness that we're limited creatures who can't do it all ourselves, who need God's help. It's a prayer of total humility.

> Because we are humans, we are also weak;
> because we are weak, we pray.
> — St. Augustine

The other kind of prayer that involves asking is called intercessory prayer: prayer in which we pray for the needs of others. Abraham prayed for the lives of the people in Sodom (cf. Genesis 18:22-32). Paul begins and ends all of his letters reminding his readers how he's praying for them and asking for their prayers, too.

So, we pray for ourselves. We pray for others. That sounds good, but we still haven't answered a question we posed way back at the beginning of this chapter. Why offer these kinds of prayers? Doesn't God know what He's doing without us?

Of course He does. But as we said before, He's set up the world so that it rolls along, grows and changes with our help. He loves through

our love. He creates through our sexuality. He heals through our hands. And, as we've seen earlier, He works through our spiritual activity as well. That's called prayer. The great writer C.S. Lewis has a lot to say about this:

> The efficacy of prayer is, at any rate, no more of a problem than the efficacy of all human acts; i.e., if you say, "it is useless to pray because Providence already knows what is best and will certainly do it," then why is it not equally useless (and for the same reason) to try to alter the course of events in any way whatever?
>
> — LETTERS; 2/21/32

> It may be a mystery why He should have allowed us to cause real events at all; but it is no odder that He should allow us to cause them by praying than by any other method.
>
> — "WORK AND PRAYER," *GOD IN THE DOCK*

Another point Lewis makes might help you understand this a little better. Or it might send you into greater depths of perplexity. Let's try it and see what happens.

We have to remember that God exists outside of space and time. Completely. Now, if you start thinking about this too hard, you might feel your brain kind of fold up and beg for mercy, but stick with it for just a second.

When you think of life chugging along in time, as it does for us, you can see how intercessory prayer can, indeed, be a little problematic. What — God's going to do one thing, and then we pray, so He does an about-face and changes course? That can't be right. But what if you think about it this way:

> We have long since agreed that if our prayers are granted at all, they are granted from the foundation of the world. God and His acts are not in time. Intercourse between God and man occurs at particular moments for the man,

I Don't Need to Pray Because . . .

but not for God. If there is — as the very concept of prayer presupposes — an adaptation between the free actions of men in prayer and the course of events, this adaptation is from the beginning inherent in the great single creative act. Our prayers are heard — don't say "have been heard" or you are putting God into time — not only before we make them but before we are made ourselves.
> — C.S. LEWIS, *LETTERS TO MALCOLM: CHIEFLY ON PRAYER*

Wow. Chew on that for a while. Now doesn't that force your sense of prayer to grow leaps and bounds beyond "Dear God, please make the pimple on my nose go away before morning?" Doesn't it, in fact, bestow a kind of awesome dignity, richness, and even power on your prayer? You're here, on your knees, praying as the seconds on your Mickey Mouse clock tick by, but in God's time, you're working with Him at the moment of creation, when there is no time. Gulp.

> ... pray for one another, that you may be healed. The fervent prayer of a righteous person is very powerful.
> — James 5:16

Let's put all the kinds of prayer we've learned about together for a minute: praise, petition, and intercession. You can probably see how any one of these can't stand alone, if you want to have an authentic, mature relationship with God (aka spirituality). Praising God leads to a deep appreciation of all He's made, including other people, which leads you to be more sensitive to their needs. It becomes impossible not to pray for them, just as it becomes impossible not to become more aware of your own smallness before God and need for God to fill in the empty spaces in your life and forgive your stupid, idiotic sins.

Those prayers of intercession and petition are going to be affected by your praise of God in another way, too. The closer you get to God,

the more you appreciate God for Who He Is, the more your needs and desires are going to mirror His.

Think about close friends, or solid, intimate married couples. Sure, they have their differences, but the closer they are, the more of one mind they become. That's the way it is when you're close to God.

As you grow more intimate with God, what you will find is that your prayers of intercession and petition change. Knowing, believing, and really accepting His Lordship over your life and all of creation, deeply trusting that He loves you, you will start one day — without even really knowing it — paying a little bit more attention to something Jesus says in the Lord's Prayer:

> . . . *Thy will be done, on earth as it is in heaven.*

You're no longer fighting God, trying to make Him do what you want. You're accepting what happens, and your main prayer transforms into one that asks God for nothing more than understanding and perhaps strength to endure. Again, our friend C.S. Lewis makes the point:

> To be in the state in which you are so at one with the will of God that you wouldn't want to alter the course of events even if you could is certainly a very high or advanced condition.
>
> — "WORK AND PRAYER," *GOD IN THE DOCK*

Not many of us are there, it's true. But maybe, through prayer, we'll get there someday.

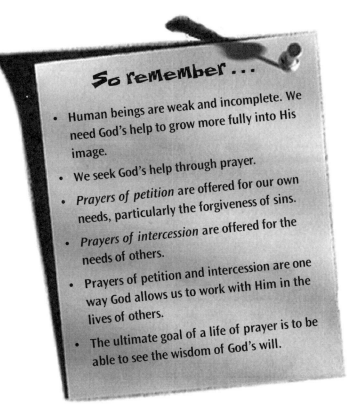

So remember . . .

- Human beings are weak and incomplete. We need God's help to grow more fully into His image.

- We seek God's help through prayer.

- *Prayers of petition* are offered for our own needs, particularly the forgiveness of sins.

- *Prayers of intercession* are offered for the needs of others.

- Prayers of petition and intercession are one way God allows us to work with Him in the lives of others.

- The ultimate goal of a life of prayer is to be able to see the wisdom of God's will.

I Want to Pray,
But It's Difficult
Because . . .

CHAPTER 4

I Want to Pray, But It's Difficult Because...

... I'm Too Busy

I KNOW YOU'RE BUSY. Believe me, I know.

Most teens and young people really are incredibly busy. You've got school, of course — seven or eight hours of undiluted fun that it is. Then there's sports. Or drama. Or music. Or your job. Or volunteer work. Or church youth group. Or maybe all of the above.

Oh, and did we mention the fact that you're part of a family, and that family actually expects you to — well — participate? That means you have work around the house. Not only do you have to clean your own personal room, but you're also responsible for anything else on your parents' list this week: kitchen cleaning, garbage organizing, lawn mowing, leaf raking, snow shoveling, babysitting, and dog walking.

Finally, somewhere in those twenty-four hours called a "day," you have to squeeze in homework and maybe one or two things you'd actually like to do: hang out with your friends, catch a little television, play on the computer, go shopping.

And now we want you to pray? Every day?

I can see why you're laughing, crying, or perhaps both. I have deep and total respect for your crazy life, and my determination to get you to pray every single day isn't rooted in an evil desire to make your life even crazier.

It's the opposite, in fact. It's about making it less crazy.

We have to be careful here. Prayer is absolutely not one more self-help trick. We're not presenting a solution to your problems, a surefire

way to help you feel better about yourself, or the key to fast and easy weight loss. Not at all. You really have to walk carefully when you think about prayer, and not fall into the trap of seeing it in purely utilitarian terms, turning to God because of what it's going to do for you and your well-being.

That kind of attitude is actually just about half a step forward from praying to God every night that you'll get a pony for Christmas. And half a step isn't very far.

So, no. We're not insisting that you turn to God every day so you can attempt to use God. (That would be a massive waste of time anyway, to tell the truth, so you might as well just skip that pointless stage of spiritual development.) We're insisting that you turn to God because that's where you belong.

We've been through some of this before. You're made by God and for God. Your only true happiness comes when you live your life in reference to God, not just on Sundays, but every minute of every day. Prayer is the road to doing just that.

Prayer must be always marked by ". . . a desire to encounter God and to make this will and his love our own. It is a search for the living God. We do not pray in order to improve our talents, to develop more clearly an intellectual synthesis, or widen our culture, religious or otherwise. We pray in order to tell God once again that we love him and know that he loves us, and to relate ourselves to the plan of mercy that is his."

— Bernard Bro, O.P.,
The Rediscovery of Prayer

So how can you *not* have time for that? The One who made and loves you is with you all the time, waiting for your conscious connection and your love. Why would you not want to hook up with Him?

Well, there is a reason, and maybe you've figured it out by now.

You've probably noticed that there is this thing called sin in the world. It's pretty awful. We may use the image of the devil in a joking way sometimes, but really and truly, there's nothing funny about sin.

There's nothing amusing about murder or terrorism, about child abuse, the Holocaust, or theft. If you've ever been lied to, if you've ever been used, if you've ever been a victim of sin, you may recall that you didn't spend much time laughing in the aftermath.

So why do people sin? The reasons for complex sins may be complex, but I really think that in the end, all sin, big and small (if there is such a thing as a "small sin" anyway), comes down to one thing: being guided by something else other than God.

It may be a desire for revenge or pleasure. It may be selfishness. It may be greed, power, or lust. Whatever the specifics, the truth is that when we sin, we have let something else inside or outside of us be our guide. We've either ignored the voice of God in our conscience or not taken time to listen for it.

If you search your own life for sinful moments, you'll probably find this is true.

So what does this have to do with being — ahem — too busy to pray?

It's actually rather simple. Frightening, but simple.

There is something out there that does not want you to pray. It wants you, in fact, to do anything else but pray. It will do all it can to distract you, entice you, seduce you, and argue you away from prayer.

Why? Because that something — that evil, that darkness — doesn't want you to listen to God.

And if you don't pray, the odds of you not listening to God are much, much higher.

That something — called the devil, in case you haven't figured it out yet — doesn't want you to be in touch with the God who loves you passionately, wants the best for you, and gives you the strength to find what is best. He doesn't want you to be in touch with the good, the true, the beautiful, and the holy.

He wants you to feel alone in the universe, to doubt whether your life has meaning, to wonder why on earth you were created, and to be convinced that there's no way to know what's really true or good.

That's exactly what he wants: for you to walk around in a daze, not being able to recognize God's voice when it echoes love and goodness, not being able to respond to the tugs on your conscience, not developing a sense of your place in God's creation.

And a great way for him to do this is to convince you that you just don't have the time to pray.

Here's what I think. Whenever I approach prayer time, and I feel that tug in another direction, that little nagging sense that says, *Not now . . . later. Don't have time. I'm feeling okay . . . no need to pray . . .* I immediately — and I mean immediately — close my eyes, open my heart, and listen. Why? Because I figure if darkness is telling me not

to listen, God must have something important to tell me that darkness doesn't want me to hear.

So sure you're busy. We all are. You're probably always going to be busy, too. Maybe even for the rest of your life.

But are you going to always be too busy to pray?

That's what *someone* would like you to think.

Still too busy?

So remember...

- Our lives are filled with activity, yet we always seem to find time for what's important.
- Prayer is important because it takes us to the heart of God, which is where we belong and where we find lasting happiness and peace.
- If you think you're too busy to pray, that makes someone very happy. And that someone isn't God.
- In *The Screwtape Letters*, C.S. Lewis wrote an imaginary correspondence from the Devil to his nephew Wormwood, who is doing the Devil's work on earth, trying to tempt a man away from "the Enemy" (God, of course):

  The best thing, where it is possible, is to keep the patient from the serious intention of praying altogether... Whenever they are attending to the Enemy Himself we are defeated, but there are ways of preventing them from doing so... Whenever there is prayer, there is danger of His own immediate action.

CHAPTER 5

I Want to Pray, But It's Difficult Because...

...I Don't Know Where to Start

THERE'S A RATHER INTRIGUING person who recently transferred to your school. He's friendly, and interesting. You've heard that, just like you, he has a keen interest in the 1989 Oakland Raiders or the frescoes of Fra Angelico or the artistry of Jim Morrison, or whatever currently obsesses you — just plug it in, and you get the point.

The point being that this smart, funny, and good-natured new guy seems to be a potential friend.

What do you do? Do you read up on his background, talk to those who know him, or just study him from afar, observing how other people interact with him?

I hope not. You might just get arrested doing that, you know.

The fact is, if you want to know someone better, you do none of these things. Instead you do something quite reasonable: You actually introduce yourself. You chat. You spend time together. And the rest will be history — of some sort or another.

And yes, it's the same with God. As we've already pointed out many times, if we want to be friends with God, a great way to start is to see Him the same way we see our human friends, and apply the demands of human friendships and relationship to our relationship with God.

So — God intrigues you. You have a sense that there's a void within you that only He can fill. You know this, not only because

people have told you it's true, but because you've experienced it. You've enjoyed great happiness and satisfaction in your life, but it always seems to fade. Even your best friends aren't there all the time, and won't be there the rest of your life. Why, you have to wonder, would God create you with a desire for happiness, peace, purpose, and wholeness, if He didn't also provide a way to find those things, not just for the moment, but for the rest of your life and forever?

Yup. God must be the one.

> **Beginners would be taught to draw near to God so that God in turn may draw near to them.**
>
> — St. Thérèse of Lisieux

But how do you start? Do you need to check out a million books from the library? Should you commit to reading the Bible from beginning to end? Should you plan on being in church every day for a while? Is that what it takes?

Not really. But there's one thing it does take:

Time.

And please don't tell me you don't have any. We'll go into this a bit more later, but if you're honest, you'll admit that there's actually a lot of wasted time in your life. You'll also admit that, like the rest of us, somehow, you always find time, in the midst of your crazy, terribly busy schedule, for the things that are important to you, such as meals, video games, talking on the phone, watching television, and even doing a little homework.

So yes, there is time. If you're really interested, you'll find time.

And that, in a nutshell, is the answer to your question of how to start:

Decide to start praying more, and commit to it.

I know you probably don't want to hear it, but the truth is, it's really best if you just go ahead and make a schedule for this adven-

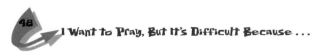

ture, even if it's only in your head. We'd like to think that we can develop a relationship with God being all casual and spontaneous, being lifted up into ecstasy when the moment seizes us, no matter where we are. But admit it. That's not going to work. You're just going to have to make an internal commitment to tend to this relationship at a certain time, in a certain place, every day, or else the rush of events and most people's natural inclinations to procrastination are going to take over.

So start there: ten minutes. When is it going to be? In the morning, before school? Right after school, when you're home alone and the house is quiet? Before you go to bed? Figure that out first. Everyone's different, so there are no rules to worry about. Decide for yourself, right now, when your ten minutes of prayer time is going to happen, every day, no matter what.

Got it? There. See how easy that was?

Now, what are you going to do during those ten minutes? Again, that's up to you, and perhaps in reading this book, you'll discover a

prayer style or type that fits your personality right now, and that would be good to start with. Or perhaps you already know — you really want to pray the Rosary. Or you just want to quietly examine your conscience and go over the day that's either coming or has just passed. If you're fairly certain, then cement it in your mind. Say, "Every morning at 7:15, I'm going to pray a decade of the Rosary," or "Every evening at 9:50, I'm going to quietly lay out the day's happenings before God." Maybe you could write a little note to yourself and stick it on your mirror or next to your alarm clock.

Not that you are destined to pray that kind of prayer for the rest of your life, or even for the rest of the month. And that's certainly not going to be the only kind of prayer you engage in during the course of a day. I hope not, at least. I hope your day is going to gradually fill up with little relaxed moments of praise, thanksgiving, and just being aware of God's presence in the joy and the muck you call your amazing life.

> It is essential to begin the practice of prayer
> with a firm resolution of persevering in it.
> — St. Teresa of Ávila

But the place all of that will start is in your commitment to some structured prayer time, easing yourself into the habit of prayer with the fewest distractions possible. It's sort of like the first few weeks of school in a new school. You have a lot to concentrate on — like surviving academically and socially. Having a set schedule makes it all easier. You'd probably fall completely apart in a quivering mess in the hallways if, in addition to the things you need to concentrate on, the class schedule changed every day, or your classes floated around to different rooms.

Right now, you're just trying to get into the habit and figure out what this prayer thing is all about. It's best to keep it simple.

Now, if you're clueless about what kind of prayer to pursue, let me make a suggestion. Get yourself a Bible and open it up to the Gospel

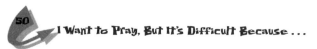

of John, Chapter 14. Make that the focus of your first adventures in prayer, and plan to spend your prayer minutes doing something like this:

Quiet yourself.

Say a short prayer of thanks and praise.

Read a couple of verses of John's Gospel.

Try not to analyze. Just let thinking happen.

Connect what you've read and thought about to something in your life.

Listen without straining to hear.

Tell God of any needs you have.

Say an Our Father or any other prayer you like and have memorized.

Say "Amen."

And yes, you can do all of that in ten minutes. If you're wondering how to do any of the specific things on the list — such as "quieting yourself" after a full day of school, softball practice, chores, and screaming siblings — don't worry. We'll cover all of that in the next few chapters.

> How does a person begin to pray? I repeat:
> What is important, is to have a firm reso-
> lution, an absolute, unshakable determina-
> tion, not to stop until one reaches the
> fountainhead, no matter what may happen
> or may enter into our lives, and no matter
> what it may cost us.
> — St. Teresa of Ávila, *Way of Perfection*

Ten minutes is not very long, and taking a bit longer to pray is better, of course, just as a thirty-minute conversation with a friend is better than ten minutes. But ten is an excellent start, and you'll probably

find that before you know it, your prayer time will lengthen without any effort.

So there's the answer to your question. You didn't know where to start, and now you do: with a promise, and with a little bit of time.

So remember...

- The first step in deepening your prayer life is... praying.
- Because we routinely put so many obstacles in the way of giving time to God in prayer, it's best to make a conscious commitment to prayer.
- The commitment should be specific about when, where, and how you're going to pray.
- Keep it simple. God doesn't want complexity, and God isn't impressed by lots of words. He just wants you.

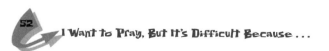

CHAPTER 6

I Want to Pray, But It's Difficult Because...

...Meditation is Weird

THERE'S A SIMPLE ANSWER to the statement above: No, it's not.

The idea of meditation might seem strange to you because you associate it with unfamiliar religions such as Hinduism or Buddhism. Or perhaps you immediately think of people engaging in contemplation while contorted into deeply uncomfortable positions. You might think meditation is all about trances and otherworldliness and escape.

I repeat: It's not.

Many modern people do, indeed, associate meditation only with Eastern religions, but it's really not correct to do so. Catholics have a deep tradition of meditative prayer, so don't believe anyone who tries to tell you that either of these two statements is true:

- If you really want to meditate, you need to get into those Eastern methods.
- You really shouldn't want to meditate, because it's going to lead you down dangerous, non-Christian paths.

Both of those assertions are absolutely false. Meditation is a type of prayer that has deep Christian roots. You don't need Eastern methods to meditate, and you don't need to be afraid of meditation, either. Everything I'm going to tell you in this chapter is from Catholic Christian sources. Saints. The *Catechism of the Catholic Church*. Even more saints. Can't get less weird or more Christian than that, if you ask me.

First, some definitions. In the last chapter I offered you a little program of prayer to get you started. Did you know that was a form of meditation? Hah. Got you!

There are lots of people who study prayer and spirituality, and these people have teased apart all different types and levels of Christian meditation techniques, but we're going to keep it simple, and stick with what the *Catechism of the Catholic Church* says about it:

> Meditation is above all a quest. The mind seeks to understand the why and how of the Christian life, in order to adhere and respond to what the Lord is asking. The required attentiveness is difficult to sustain. We are usually helped by books . . . the Sacred Scriptures, particularly the Gospels, holy icons . . . works of spirituality, the great book of creation, and that of history —- the page on which the "today" of God is written.
>
> To meditate on what we read helps us to make it our own by confronting it with ourselves. Here, another book is opened: the book of life. We pass from thoughts to reality. . . .
>
> — Nos. 2705-2706

> Meditation is a prayerful quest engaging thought, imagination, emotion, and desire. Its goal is to make our own in faith the subject considered, by confronting it with the reality of our own life.
>
> — No. 2723

So in meditation, what happens is this: Our spirits engage with something external that reveals God to us: Scripture, other writings, a symbol of God, or nature. That interaction orients us toward God and opens our hearts to Him. In the process — or "quest" as the *Catechism* calls it — the subject of our meditation becomes a part of us, and we're alert to God's presence within.

Contemplative prayer is an even deeper form of this kind of interior prayer. Contemplative prayer is a purer kind of communion with God, in which there aren't any external aids to prayer, simply the one praying and God, in an intense communion of love. As the *Catechism* says:

> Contemplative prayer is the simple expression of the mystery of prayer. It is a gaze of faith fixed on Jesus, an attentiveness to the Word of God, a silent love. It achieves real union with the prayer of Christ to the extent that it makes us share in his mystery.
>
> — *CCC*, No. 2724

Maybe a good way to think about it is this: Meditation is like a conversation between you and your best friend about a really good movie you've just seen. Talking about the movie helps you both to reveal

more about yourselves and learn something, and the sharing deepens the connection between the two of you. Contemplation is like the last moment you saw your best friend, right before you moved away. You looked at each other, and there was really nothing to say. No words could express how you felt. All you could do was just be there, deep in your friendship and all that it was at that moment.

Right now, meditation is the prayer for you. You may indeed enjoy flashes of contemplative moments here and there, but you shouldn't see such moments as a goal. Prayer isn't like school, a place where your goal is to pass through various stages and classes in order to get a diploma or a degree. You shouldn't see your prayer life as a successions of achievements brought about by your praiseworthy efforts. You're not taking time for meditative prayer because you want to become some big hot-shot contemplative. You're doing it because you love God. Somewhere along the line, you might be gifted with a deeper awareness, but that's what it will be: a gift. When we're learning about prayer, we have to walk a really fine line. There are certain things we have to learn about it. There are certain "techniques" that will help us. But in the end, what we're talking about is nothing more than learning how to get out of the way so God can tell us how much He loves us.

Learning to pray is really, in the end, about learning to do nothing, and letting God do everything.

> . . . prayer places our intellect in the brilliance of God's light and exposes our will to the warmth of his heavenly love. . . . It is a stream of holy water that flows forth and makes the plants of our good desires grow green and flourish and quenches the passions within our hearts.
>
> — St. Francis de Sales,
> *Introduction to the Devout Life*

 I Want to Pray, But It's Difficult Because . . .

In the previous chapter, I offered you a little sketch of how to begin to meditate. Now I'm going to offer you another, more detailed sketch, but this one isn't mine. It's from someone a lot smarter: St. Francis de Sales.

St. Francis de Sales was a bishop who lived in the sixteenth century. He did a lot of great things, like helping Catholics who were oppressed by Calvinist Protestants maintain their faith. He also wrote — so much, in fact, that he's the patron saint of writers and journalists. More than anything else, St. Francis de Sales wrote about spirituality.

The great thing about St. Francis de Sales for us is that unlike so many other spiritual writers of the past, he wrote about prayer and the spiritual life not for monks and nuns, but for ordinary lay people living out in the world, people with families and kids and jobs. He understood the distractions and challenges that such a life poses to trying to nurture prayer, but just as importantly, he understood what happens to us when we ignore the spiritual and cut ourselves off from God: We're literally wasting our lives.

Here's the pattern for meditation that St. Francis de Sales laid out in his book *Introduction to the Devout Life*, a book originally written for a lay woman seeking his advice in prayer. He calls this person "Philothea" . . . "a soul loving, or in love, with, God."

Here's what he tells her to do:

Prepare

We prepare for prayer in two ways. First, we place ourselves in God's presence in whatever way works best for us. We can simply take a few minutes to quiet ourselves and bring that thought to mind, or we can even use our imaginations, picturing Jesus sitting next to us, ready to listen. In the next chapter, we're going to talk about techniques to help concentration during prayer. This is where those techniques would come in.

Secondly, we prepare by asking God to help us. It's simple, but important. When we start thinking about prayer as dependent on our

work, skills, or effort, we're in trouble. As Paul says, we "do not pray as we ought," and this amazing act of opening ourselves to the holy presence of God requires a lot of help. St. Francis suggests praying a line from a Psalm:

> *Give me insight to observe your teaching,*
> *to keep it with all my heart.* (PSALM 119:34)

> *Let your face shine upon your servant;*
> *teach me your laws.*
> (PSALM 119:135)

Or even the words of the apostles to Jesus:

> *Lord, teach us to pray . . .* (LUKE 11:1)

The Interior Lesson

After you've readied yourself and asked for God's help, read the Scripture or other reading that's the focus of your prayer. Or focus on the picture of Jesus or crucifix that you're using. Then, St. Francis suggests,

I Want to Pray, But It's Difficult Because . . .

use your imagination to connect to the mystery. If you've read part of the Sermon on the Mount, read it again, imagining Jesus speaking those words on the hillside, and imagine yourself there.

St. Francis suggests the use of the imagination here as a way to minimize distractions. He says, "By such imaginative means we restrict our mind to the mystery on which we meditate so that it will not wander about, just as we cage a bird or put a leash on a hawk so he can rest on our hand."

Considerations

This is where your thinking comes in. You've invited God in and used your imagination to bring the reality of God's love close to you. Now it's time to let God speak through your intellect about what you've encountered. Let St. Francis tell you how to do it. He does a much better job than I could:

"If your mind finds enough appeal, light, and fruit in any of them, remain with that point and do not go on any further. Imitate the bees, who do not leave a flower as long as they can extract any honey out of it. But if you do not come on anything that appeals to you after you have examined and tried it for a while, then go on to another, but proceed calmly and simply in this matter and do not rush yourself."

Do you get that? Relax. Don't stress. Don't look for answers or try to achieve anything. Trust God.

Resolutions

This is the part of prayer that leads to action — we hope. After encountering the love of God, seeing how it's at work in your life and seeing how it could be at work, you will probably be moved to some sort of action: to nurture your love for God even more, to share that love, or even something more specific, such as cleaning up the mess remaining from that stupid string of lies you told about your history homework, or being brave and actually stopping to talk to that kid everyone one makes fun of for no reason.

... Meditation is Weird

59

Conclusion

St. Francis suggests that we end our prayer with three acts: a prayer of thanksgiving to God for His mercy and love, an offering of our own resolutions in union with God's love, and prayers of petition and intercession.

There. It sounds complicated at first, but it's really not. And it's definitely not weird.

You may be asking — why the structure?

The structure is there, quite simply, for the reason that structure is a part of many aspects of life. We need it. We're distractible, fickle creatures. You know that any one of us can come up with a huge list of reasons not to pray at all, or not to pray at this moment, or to put it off just one more day. The structure provided to us by experienced pray-ers strengthens us so that we're less tempted by those excuses.

This particular structure isn't carved in any kind of stone, of course. As you journey closer to God, you should be experimenting with various ways of praying, seeing what works for you and what doesn't. Just remember: This is not a test. This is not a class. There's no pressure to succeed or excel — it's all about finding the space in your heart where you can most clearly hear the Good News of God's love for you.

> Therefore my advice to you, friends, is turn aside from troubled and anxious reflection on your own progress, and escape to the easier path of remembering the good things which God has done; in this way, instead of becoming upset by thinking about yourself, you will find relief by turning your attention to God. . . .
>
> — St. Bernard of Clairvaux,
> *Sermon on the Song of Songs*

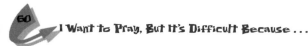

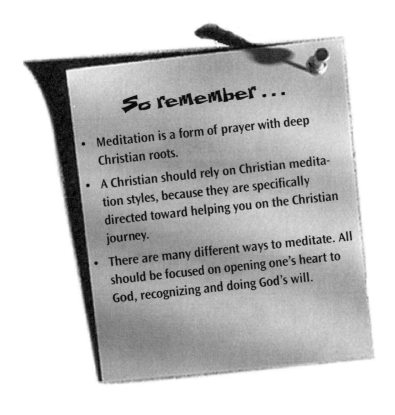

So remember...

- Meditation is a form of prayer with deep Christian roots.
- A Christian should rely on Christian meditation styles, because they are specifically directed toward helping you on the Christian journey.
- There are many different ways to meditate. All should be focused on opening one's heart to God, recognizing and doing God's will.

CHAPTER 7

I Want to Pray, But It's Difficult Because...

...I Can't Concentrate

YOUR FRIEND HAS SOMETHING really important to say to you.

You can tell, because all night long at the party, he's been signaling you, whispering, "We really have to talk," when he passes by, and — this worries you a little bit — looking more than a touch depressed.

So, you've finally torn yourself away from The Guy Who's Memorized Last Spring's Baseball Season In Incredible Detail, and found your friend. He's relieved. He starts talking.

What's he saying? Well, to tell the truth, you're not exactly sure. See, you guys are standing right next to the DJ, and music is blasting, so you're really only catching every other word. Plus, you can't help looking at your watch — there is that curfew you really, really can't break this week. Plus, Baseball Guy brought a whole lot of worries to your mind that you just can't shake — worries about getting in shape for track season (no disrespect to Baseball Guy, but it's just really not your sport), and worries about that pre-calculus grade, which is not exactly the best and is threatening to make you ineligible for the team.

The end result?

You aren't listening. Because of the music, you can't hear the words your friend is saying clearly, and your mind is so cluttered with other pressures that you can't really hear even the random words that you happen to catch between songs.

The solution is obvious: move away from the deafening music and deal with the mental distractions. There are a couple of ways you could do this. You could forcibly eject them from your consciousness, or, if your conversation takes a leisurely turn, you could mention the time pressure or that you're worried about your math grade. Either way, you're going to clear up some mental space that you can now devote to your friend.

Distractions are really common obstacles to prayer. You're not alone in discovering this. The best way to deal with them is to view them in much the same way as you'd see the distractions during that incredibly difficult party conversation.

> Beginners must accustom themselves to pay no heed to what they see or hear, and they must practice doing this during hours of prayer.
>
> — St. Teresa of Ávila

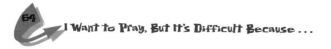

First, there was all that noise. If your concentration is broken by external distractions such as noise or music, do what you did at that party. Move your body somewhere else. Turn the music off. Choose another prayer time when your house isn't quite so chaotic. Give up on your fantasy of private prayer time in the bedroom you share with your brother and apparently half of his second-grade class. Go to the back yard. Unless it's snowing. Then go someplace else.

Now what about those pesky internal distractions? What to do about them?

The first step is to prepare your body and soul for prayer. Just think about any other time you're about to do something that requires a lot of concentration — writing a paper or taking an important exam. Do you just walk in from attending a football game where you've been screaming for three hours, sit down, and start writing? Maybe, but if you do, what comes out is probably going to be fairly garbled. No, before you embark on a task that takes focus, you take a few minutes and ... well ... focus.

There are lots of different ways to prepare yourself to focus on prayer, and most of them involve both your body and your spirit. Why? Because the two are connected. You're not preparing to meet God as some disembodied spirit — you're preparing to meet God as you: a human being knit of both body and soul. Prayer involves both.

> May the God of peace himself make you perfectly holy and may you entirely, spirit, soul, and body, be preserved blameless for the coming of our Lord Jesus Christ.
> — 1 Thessalonians 5:23

First, sit up. I don't care where — on the floor, on your bed, in a pew in a chapel. Wherever you are, just sit up. Don't lie down. No matter how tired you are, don't. You may reason that you want to be relaxed during prayer, and what's more relaxing than lying down, and

there's your problem. If you lie down, you'll probably relax yourself right into sleep, and it's not quite time for that yet. So wake up and sit up.

(Or stand, kneel, or even walk. Just don't — you heard me — don't lie down!)

Now it's time to quiet your soul and clear a little space in it where your time with God can begin. A couple of suggestions for doing this:

Work with your muscles and nerves. Starting with your toes, take a few seconds to focus on the individual parts of your body. Think of this as either "concentrating on" that part or "relaxing" it. Work your way up slowly, and by the time you're up to your ears, you'll probably feel like you're floating. See why I said not to lie down?

Work with your eyes and focus on an object. Use a crucifix or a picture of Jesus. A candle is a popular choice, especially when you link it to a prayer asking Jesus to overcome whatever darkness is inside you. A vast night sky full of billions of stars, a huge ocean crammed with millions of creatures, or even just a bird sitting on a fence minding its own God-given business can help focus your mind on the amazing fact that the God who's mighty enough to put all of this together cares about you and wants to know what's up in your life tonight.

Work with your breath. Here, you can either focus on your breathing (although some people say this makes them just breathe faster) or you can gradually slow down your breathing pace, accompanying each breath with a little prayer. Some suggestions:

"Jesus."

"Jesus, I love you."

"God is love."

"Lord Jesus Christ, have mercy on me, a sinner."

"In him we live and move and have our being."

That last phrase is from Scripture (Acts 17:28), and there are lots of other phrases in the Bible you could choose. The second-to-the-last phrase actually has a name. It's called the "Jesus Prayer," and is rooted

in Eastern Orthodox Christianity, where it's repeated by some believ-
ers hundreds of times a day.

All this talk about focusing your breath and repeating a phrase
may prompt you to think that we're borrowing a page from Eastern
religions such as Hinduism or Buddhism here. Not really. Eastern religions may get all the good press these days, but Christian meditation
has roots just as deep. If you decide to do more research into these
kinds of prayer techniques, you might be tempted to look at books
coming at it from the perspective of Eastern religions. Don't.

It's not that it would be a big enormous sin, but it is a waste of
time. Eastern meditation has a different ultimate purpose than Christian meditation. The Eastern ways really come down to manipulating
your body and mind into a certain state. It's more psychological. In
the Catholic Christian tradition of prayer, we do some of the same
things as the Easterners, but for a different reason: to open our spirits to a deeper relationship with God. To make room for Him to dwell
within us.

Okay, so you've done all this, you've read some Scripture, said a bit of the Rosary, and now you're opening yourself to God. What? Is there a problem?

Oh — that chemistry test tomorrow. The weird way your supposedly best friend acted after school. Your stupid job that you thought was so cool at first, but that you now hate.

Can't get them off your mind, can you? You spiritual slacker, you. You must be doing something wrong.

Actually, no. What you're experiencing is perfectly natural. But if you're faced with these kinds of distractions, don't try to fight them. Do not sit there all uptight, squeezing your eyes shut even tighter, and vowing, "I will not think about the test. I will not think about the test. I will not ..."

No, this is obviously not going to work, just like it doesn't work when you're trying to get in shape and all you can think about is ice cream. Or just like it doesn't work when all of Jill's friends are sitting at a table at lunch, and all of Jill's friends have just seen Jill's "boyfriend," Jack, holding hands with Little Bo Peep in the hallway, and no one wants to mention it, but nothing else meaningful can be said because the sight of Jack holding hands with Peep was just too wretched.

You know how it goes, don't you? The more we try to avoid a topic, the heavier it weighs in our souls.

The way to deal with all of these distractions in life or in prayer is not to fight them, but, as you did with your friend, bring them out in the open and make them a part of the conversation.

After all, you're not praying to escape from your life. You're praying so that you can see God more clearly in every part of your life. If something is weighing on your mind, it's pretty clear that what we have here is an issue that needs God's attention.

Say it's a person you're concerned about: your sick grandfather, your broken-hearted friend, or your obnoxious locker mate. Stop

stressing, stop fuming, and pray for that person. Ask God to be with the sick or hurting person. Pray that the obnoxious locker mate will find peace, because he's obviously in need of it. Pray for patience and wisdom in dealing with that person.

What if it's a problem that's bugging you? You're suffering from unrequited love. Your stomach starts churning with dread an hour before you have to go to work, without fail, every day. You have three papers due in a week, and there is no way you are ever going to get them done unless you grow an extra brain and two more pairs of hands in the next twenty-four hours. Your mom and dad will not stop fighting. Ever.

> I have many distractions, but as soon as I am aware of them, I pray for those people the thought of whom is diverting my attention. In this way, they reap the benefit of my distractions.
> — St. Thérèse of Lisieux

Take one or any of those issues that won't leave you alone and bring them to God in the prayer. Tell God, in total honesty how you feel about it. Cry if you have to. Pound a pillow. Write it out in a journal, if that's your thing. However you choose, just let it all out in God's presence.

You see, the point of prayer is not to shut life out. It's the exact opposite: Through intimacy with God, we live our lives more deeply. Sometimes the distractions we experience in prayer are silly and hardly worth a thought. But sometimes distractions aren't distractions at all — they're what we should be praying about in the first place.

So remember . . .

- Distractions during prayer are normal.
- You can minimize external distractions by your choices of where and how to pray.
- You can minimize internal distractions by using your body and mind to calm yourself and create a quiet space.
- If you're distracted by a problem or a concern, bring that distraction to God in prayer. If it's on your mind, it's obviously something you need to pray about.

 I Want to Pray, But It's Difficult Because . . .

CHAPTER 8

I Want to Pray, But It's Difficult Because...

... The Bible is Too Hard to Read

HERE'S A SCENARIO for you:

Your friend of one day is sitting with you at lunch, studying you intently. To be honest, it's making you a little nervous, and you wish he'd just stop and finish his Ruffles. But then, finally, he speaks.

"I've decided," he announces, "that your name is Fred."

"But it's not," you protest, more than a little puzzled, although not exactly brimming with pride about the truth. "It's Alphonsus."

Undeterred, your friend is continuing. "And you love soccer, mocha ice cream, and techno music. You hope to graduate, move to Alaska, and spend the rest of your life studying moose antlers."

What's going on? (Besides the fact that your "friend" has apparently chosen this moment to reveal his inner whacked-out self.) Why is this guy making totally ungrounded pronouncements about your identity? He hasn't had the chance to get to know you yet, to find out that you absolutely hate soccer, are allergic to anything with coffee in it, and haven't been able to listen to techno since that girl you dated dropped you for the DJ at KlubKlepto. Not to mention that it's not moose antlers. It's elk antlers, bozo.

"Why are you saying that stuff? That's not me at all!" you protest.

The friend shrugs. "Sure it is," he responds as he tosses the chip bag into the trash. "I've decided that's who you are, so that's how I'm going to relate to you. And I am devoted to soccer and techno. So, see ya."

All right. This makes no sense. A person has chosen to relate to you not based on who you really are, but based on what he's made up about you. Crazy. Just crazy.

So, who is this "God" you're praying too, anyway?

Do you even know?

Or are you, like Mr. Chips, relating or not relating to God based on rumors or the fruits of your imagination?

Do you even know who you're talking to?

> Be constantly committed to prayer or to reading [Scripture]; by praying, you speak to God, in reading, God speaks to you.
> — St. Cyprian of Carthage, Ep 1, 15

This, obviously, is why the Bible is such an important part of our faith life as Catholic Christians. It's our source for knowing who this Best Friend is. Knowing God through the Scriptures is essential, especially in these days in which you're regularly told that God is whomever you want God to be.

Sorry. God is God and neither you nor I can tell Him who He is.

So yes, you should be reading the Scriptures on your own and listening carefully to the Scripture readings proclaimed at Mass to plunge more deeply into the love and mystery of the God who made you.

But this book is about prayer, not theology, so study isn't our emphasis. Using the Scriptures in prayer is. So where do you start? At the very beginning on day one, and work your way through?

Not a good idea. But neither is it a good idea to blindly open the Bible, close your eyes, point, then use whatever verse you've ended up with as a beginning for prayer. You need to have a method to your not-quite-madness.

Let's try to sort it out.

There are a number of options you could follow in your use of Scriptures in prayer. The two I cited above: starting with Genesis 1 and

working your way through, or playing the game of open-and-point, are both bad ones. You'd be better off doing one of three things at first:

You might think about following the lectionary — the readings the Church selects for use at Mass. On weekdays, there are two readings, and on Sundays, three, plus a Psalm every day. It's no big challenge to find these readings. You could ask your parish priest or youth minister if you could borrow one of the paperback missalettes in the pew. I'm sure they'd be so amazingly impressed and taken aback by your request that they'd just have to say yes. A lot of parishes also print the readings for the week in the bulletin.

There are also several little daily devotional booklets, issued either monthly or quarterly. Your parish magazine rack probably has a few stacked up for the taking.

Easiest of all is to go online. Web site addresses change all the time, so it would probably be useless for me to direct you to some current sites that feature the readings, but just do this: Go to a good search engine, enter the words "Catholic" and "lectionary" and see what pops

up. There are many sites out there that not only tell you what the readings are for each day, but offer you short meditations to go along with those readings as well.

Just be sure you do this: Stay Catholic. Yes, there are devotions for teens put out by non-Catholic publishers. Tons of them. But for now, do yourself a favor and stick with the Catholic lectionary and Catholic resources. If you decide to base your meditation time on the readings from the Catholic lectionary, you're doing a very cool thing: You're praying over the very same readings that millions of Catholics all over the world are hearing at Mass, in their own parishes, in their own languages. They're praying. You're praying. We're all praying. With the same wisdom and Word of God. It's an awesome thought.

If that doesn't appeal to you, you could work your way through a particular book of the Bible (although the lectionary readings do this much of the time anyway, particularly the readings for daily Mass). I'd

I Want to Pray, But It's Difficult Because . . .

suggest a Gospel at first — maybe the Gospel of John, just to be different. Or perhaps you could turn to one of Paul's letters. They're good because they're very personal, direct, and sometimes intense. They're not abstract at all, because Paul was dealing with the very real problems of real people he'd met. He was totally dedicated to their continuing growth in the love of Christ, and it shows. When you're reading Paul, it's not hard to imagine that he's talking straight to your own heart, even two thousand years later.

Finally, if all of that just seems to be too much for you, just turn to the back of this book. I've got a bunch of suggestions there for Scripture readings to get your started.

Got that Bible. Got a plan. Now what do you do?

As is often the case with prayer, the first thing you need to do is chill out. This isn't a competition, and it's not a test. God isn't hanging out, waiting for you to pick up that Bible and read in order to give you bad news or frustrate you.

When you're about to pray with the Word of God for the first time, relax.

Hold onto your faith that God loves you and wishes nothing but joy and wholeness for you.

Acknowledge that maybe, just maybe, you're not completely aware of how to find that deep spiritual joy yourself. Maybe God knows something you don't.

Accept the fact that one of the major ways God is going to let you know about your own personal road to truth, love, and joy is through His Word in the Scripture.

And submit yourself to that truth.

(That, in case you haven't noticed, is the really, really hard part. Thy will be done. Four little words that, more often than not, we say through gritted teeth, only half-believing what we're saying.)

So how do you start?

With a little prayer that acknowledges all those complicated truths:

Speak, for your servant is listening. (1 SAMUEL 3:10)

And then read.

And then stop.

What? You've only read a verse or two? Great. Because that's all I really want you to read right now. Okay, if it's a story, go ahead and read to the end, but whatever you do, read slowly.

Read the Scripture verses you've selected (as few as possible, really), slowly, and several times. You might even try reading them out loud. That will force you to slow down, and it might just deepen their impact, as well.

Now, remember — this is not a Bible study. You don't need to run and consult four or five commentaries to "figure out" what the passages mean. If there's a word or image that puzzles you, by all means, read the note provided in the Bible you're using. But don't get all scholarly on us here. There's a place for that, but it's not here. Sometimes too much study can have the effect of placing ourselves back into the center of our Scripture prayer, rather than clearing the way for God to use those words to speak to us. So be careful. Don't be stupid, but don't think that the expansion of your already impressive brain is the point. Listening is the point.

After you've read the passage slowly and repeatedly, stop and let God do His work. Soak in the words. Let them interact with your life. Be quiet. Meditate. Listen. If your mind starts wandering, read the passage again.

It's okay to use your imagination, too, especially if you're using a story as the focus of your prayer. If you've selected the passage from Mark 4:35-41 about Jesus, the apostles, and a really big storm, read the story verse by verse, closing your eyes after each sentence and imagining yourself in the scene. See yourself in the little boat, rocked

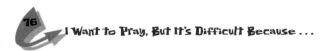

by fierce waves. See Jesus asleep in the corner and let yourself feel whatever you feel. Who knows how that will connect with your life? Maybe you're presently wondering why God seems to be asleep in relation to a particular problem you're having. Maybe you could say, along with the apostles, "Teacher, do you not care that we are perishing?" Then say it, and let the scene in the Gospel connect with your life. Listen when Jesus calms the storm, turns, looks at you and the other apostles and says, "Why are you terrified? Do you not yet have faith?"

After that kind of prayer, you'll probably be able to see why the author of the letter to the Hebrews writes:

> *Indeed, the word of God is living and effective, sharper than any two-edged sword, penetrating even between soul and spirit, joints and marrow, and able to discern reflections and thoughts of the heart.*
> *No creature is concealed from him, but everything is naked and exposed to the eyes of him to whom we must render an account.* (HEBREWS 4:12-13)

All of this can be worked into whatever type of prayer time you've settled on, which means that your Scripture meditation would end with prayers for yourself and others, as well as a sense of what you'll carry from this prayer into the rest of your day, your week and your life.

Another thing that might just come of it is that as you read the Scriptures, slowly and carefully, you'll do something you never thought you would: start remembering Scripture. Verses just might start popping into your head at strange and unexpected times during the day. You might find that when you're tempted to stress out over a test or a snub or a family crisis, bringing to mind a verse of Scripture helps you cope. Why? Because it's God speaking to you, of course.

The Word of God just might become your word, too.

> Some part of your daily reading should, each day, be stored in the stomach, that is in the memory, so that it may be digested. At times it should be brought up again for frequent rumination. You should select something that is in keeping with your calling and in line with your personal orientation, something which will seize hold of your mind and not allow it to think over alien matters.
>
> — William of St. Thierry, *Golden Epistle*

So remember . . .

- If you want to make sure your prayer is centered on God, make Scripture the center of your prayer.
- Your attitude toward the Word of God in prayer should be one of humility and submission.
- Scripture prayer is not Scripture study. Do both, but don't confuse the two.

CHAPTER 9

WHY DO WORDS become "meaningless," anyway?

Is it the words' fault, or could it possibly be the speaker's?

Consider. If you suspect that someone is speaking insincerely to you, if she's saying she likes you when she really doesn't, or he makes promises he never seems to keep, or if your parent tastes your latest kitchen creation, gets an odd smile, and murmurs, "Oh, this is really good. You did a great job on it," where do you place blame?

Do you say that words themselves have no meaning and never can again, that the phrases "Sure, we're friends, or "I'll be there, I prom-ise," or "Delicious" are suddenly without meaning, should be stricken from our conversations, never to be used again?

Probably not. You probably would be more prone to blame the person who's using those words, twisting them, or simply mouthing them without intending to convey any truth through them.

It just might be the same with prayer.

MEMORIZED PRAYERS HAVE A really bad reputation. They're for little kids who aren't smart enough to figure out what to say to God on their own. They're for the spiritually immature. God prefers us to pray "from the heart" and spontaneously.

Is that reputation deserved?

Is the practice of using memorized prayers, or even using prayers written by other people, really such a bad thing? Is it really only for little kids who don't know better?

Let's talk about talking for a minute. How many totally original, previously unheard of turns of phrase invented by you have you used today?

Waiting. Waiting.

You mean every word you've spoken has been used before by someone else? You didn't create a totally new vocabulary or phrase book every time you opened your mouth?

Well then, everything you said must have been meaningless and pointless, right?

Of course not. You probably conveyed quite a bit of meaning today, and good for you. And marvels of marvels, you did it by using words, phrases, and ideas you didn't invent yourself.

Congratulations, although we hope that next time you find another, perhaps less colorful way to tell the guy who's been bugging you for a date to leave you alone. But it worked, right?

It's not difficult to see how the same idea can apply to prayer.

We have a lot to say to God. Much of what we want to communicate is unique to who we are. The specifics of our lives can only be expressed from our hearts, using our own words.

But there's more to be expressed in prayer than the bare facts of our lives and a superficial account of our feelings. If you're a person who feels deeply and sees beyond the surface, you know that the more profound an experience or a feeling, the more difficult it is to come up with words adequate to the experience.

When you're sitting in the quiet, aware of the presence of the Creator of the universe right in your own heart, contemplating His amazing love for you, you might find words a little hard to come by. Maybe.

I Want to Pray, But It's Difficult Because . . .

And you might find it helpful to turn to the words of others who've had the same experience, shared the same yearnings, and, especially, have walked a little further down the road toward God than you have at this point.

These prayers — the Psalms, the traditional Christian prayers, the prayers written by great saints and mystics — have been the foundation of the prayer lives of most Christians for two thousand years. To reject them is to flagrantly disobey that first rule of prayer of which we spoke a while back: to pray like a poor person, in absolute humility.

As Saint Paul says, ". . . we do not know how to pray as we ought" (Romans 8:26). His point was to encourage us to depend, then, on the Holy Spirit to help us pray. That happens, in part, by using prayers that the Spirit has inspired in the hearts and minds of others.

Just remember this:

All prayer should be from the heart. Sometimes our spontaneously offered words point to what's in our hearts just fine. Sometimes words

... Memorized Prayers are Meaningless

written by others express our heart's desires, love, and need for God just as well or even better.

Here's another point: All people who speak of prayer, from Jesus on, say short and simple is best. You probably know this is true from normal human conversation as well — when someone just goes ON and ON, babbling spontaneously about how glad they are to be here judging the Fortieth Annual St. Griswald High School Bake-Off, the whole audience, you most of all (because it's your cousin doing the babbling), wishes she'd just written a few sentences on a card, said them, and taken her seat beside the brownie table.

Um, maybe God feels the same way:

> *In praying, do not babble like the pagans, who think that they will be heard because of their many words. Do not be like them. Your Father knows what you need before you ask him.*　　　　　　　　　　　　(MATTHEW 6:7-8)

And then Jesus goes on to share the words of the Lord's Prayer. All fifty-three of them.

So how should we use these prayers? Some suggestions:

1) Use memorized prayers or prayers written by others as a way to focus your heart in prayer. Pray the Lord's Prayer slowly at the beginning of your prayer time, letting the words sink into your consciousness and speak to you. If you find yourself distracted in the middle of prayer, recall yourself by saying a Hail Mary. Close your prayer time with one of these prayers. Perhaps an Act of Contrition if the need arises, or maybe a Glory Be.

2) Pray one of these prayers as the center of your prayer. Use any of the really familiar prayers, or read one that's new from a good Catholic prayer book. Pray slowly. Don't force or strain yourself, wracking your brain to search for meaning. Then you're placing yourself at the center of the prayer like an argument, instead of clearing a spot for God to touch your heart. I promise that one or two phrases will pop

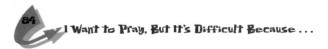
I Want to Pray, But It's Difficult Because ...

out at you. When that happens, stop, let those phrases mesh with the details of your life and who you are, and just listen.

> **It is better to say one Pater Noster fervently and devoutly than a thousand with no devotion and full of distraction.**
> — St. Edmund

3) If there's a particular emotion or circumstance that's overwhelming you, look for a prayer that fits, and use that. Spontaneously exploding at God in confusion or rage or sorrow has its purpose, and can be a good thing. But the problem is that it's just your emotions drifting around again, putting you and your efforts at the center of prayer. It's important to put those circumstances in the context of faith and point your emotions in the right direction. If you look, you'll find prayers written for every occasion you can imagine: fear, worry, sorrow for sin, love, confusion. When you plunge yourself into one of those prayers, written by the Psalmist or one of our saints or mystics, you can be assured that whatever needs you're expressing are being channeled in a way that's going to be spiritually fruitful.

These prayers may not express exactly in every detail what you want to say, but perhaps they express what you should be saying.

Finally, offer a traditional prayer when you don't feel like praying anything else. If you're just exhausted, and can't even muster the energy to brush your teeth, and know, without a doubt, that if you tried to pray for any length of time, you'd probably just topple over and start snoozing right there on the carpet, then crawl into bed, thank God for another day of life, tell God how sorry you are for whatever you did wrong, and say an Our Father. Or offer a Glory Be when, in the middle of the day, you're feeling particularly rotten about how things are going. It's a way to focus your attention on the big picture and nurture an attitude of gratitude to God for life, rather than begrudging life for seeming sort of hopeless at the moment.

... Memorized Prayers are Meaningless

If you're still not convinced, consider this.

Have you ever been in love? Or at least in deep, abiding like?

Have you ever felt absolutely clueless as to how to communicate your emotions to the Most Wonderful Person in the Universe?

What did you do? (Besides stand there with an idiotic grin on your face, of course.)

Well, you might have done one of the following things:

- Bought a card with a verse or picture that expresses how you feel.
- Cut out a cartoon from the newspaper that captures your relationship perfectly.
- Recorded a song that seemed to have been written by someone eavesdropping on your heart, then sneaked the tape or CD into Most Wonderful's locker or backpack.

See? You use other people's words all the time. You hook into their power and make them your own.

Prayers are like that. Written by other pray-ers, in love with God, shared with you, so you can make them your own, as well.

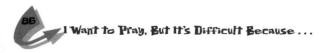

So remember . . .

- Don't dismiss memorized or written prayers as empty or useless. They're the opposite, in fact. They bear the gift of the love and yearnings of millions of Christians who have prayed them over the centuries.

- Prayers written by others give voice to our own hearts and give shape to our own needs within the framework of faith.

- Use written prayers in meditation or throughout the day.

CHAPTER 10

I Want to Pray, But It's Difficult Because ...

... I Don't Know Whether It's God I'm Hearing, or Just Me

Has this ever happened to you?

The telephone rings. You answer it, idly wondering which of your many admirers is on the line this time. The voice on the other end chirps,

"Hey, it's me. How are you doing?"

Ummm. Okay. You really don't want to be rude, but there's one problem.

You have absolutely no clue who this is. None.

Well, silly you. It's Ima Fidgett, the girl who sat behind you eight years ago in second grade! How in the world could you not know?

Easy. We don't recognize unfamiliar voices.

The opposite is true, too. When you know someone really, really well, and have spent hours talking to them, sometimes all you have to do is hear one little syllable of one word to know exactly who's called.

We recognize familiar voices.

Conversed with God lately? No? Well then, how in the world can you get all bent out of shape if His voice isn't instantly recognizable to you?

The difficult thing is, of course, that we're not talking about physical voices constructed of actual sound waves striking our ears. With

God, we're talking about something a little different, something less tangible and more challenging to hear:

A Voice that usually doesn't use a voice. Communication from Someone who doesn't use the telephone, e-mail, or sign language.

When you're praying, how can you tell the difference between God's "voice" and the flood of other voices that fill your head: your parents' lectures, your pastor's homilies, your friends' assurances, the messages of the media, and, hardest of all, your own desires and needs?

It might seem impossible — so impossible that you're tempted to give up trying and just spend the rest of your life babbling happily to yourself. But you know, recognizing God's voice isn't impossible. In fact, it's so non-impossible that there's even a word for the process, used for centuries by people who know a whole bunch about prayer:

Discernment.

Discernment is sort of the same thing as listening, only more. It's about hearing, but it's also about understanding correctly. As you

begin to journey deeper into a relationship with God, it's absolutely essential that you grasp the importance of discernment. There are lots of other voices out there competing for your attention, your will, and even your soul. Not everything that sounds comforting, reasonable, or loving is from God. As you learn to pray, you're going to learn how to be more open, but also to be more critical as well, so you're not fooled by those voices.

To start down the road of discernment, you have to understand how God works. If you think the only way to tell whether it's God speaking to you is through a voice blasting you from heaven, or dramatic acts such as blinding you or throwing you off a horse, please forget it. I mean, just forget it.

Sure, God speaks to people in those ways (except for the big, booming voice part) as well as many others, but that's for one reason and one reason only: God speaks to us ALL THE TIME in EVERYTHING WE DO.

Didn't we go through this before? I think it was back when you were arguing with me about not having to actually set aside time to pray because God's with you all the time and you can just chat. At that point, we made some excellent and irrefutable points about the difference between presence and being aware of presence.

Now, what you need to do is go back, grasp that notion of God's constant presence once again, and look at it from a different angle for a different purpose:

God is present to you all the time.

There. Here. Within. Communicating. Guiding. Loving. You.

Praying is being aware of that guiding, loving, speaking, comforting, challenging, questioning Presence, listening to it and responding to it — in praise, thanksgiving, petition, intercession, or just . . . being.

So how do you sense this pretty wonderful God-Presence? Through your spirit, of course, as God is Spirit. You sense His voice through your thoughts, your conscience, your heart, and even your imagination.

Okay, okay, you've got that part now. So let's get to it, shall we?

Your thoughts, conscience, heart, and imagination are full of quite a few other voices — voices of adults from the past and present, voices of your friends, voices of the media — how can you tell whether what you're hearing is the voice of God?

There are two parts to discernment. The first is all about you, and your readiness to listen. It's what you have to be.

After all, how much are you going to learn in English class if you've decided the teacher's dumb, you despise him, English literature is pointless, and school is even worse? Not much.

Have you ever had a conversation with your parents that seemed to be absolutely, totally worthless because they'd decided what they thought long before you even walked in the room to start the discussion?

When you're closed-minded, you're not going to learn or understand, and there's a lot you might not even hear.

So it is with God.

If you want to discern God's voice in your prayer and in your life, it would be good if you'd work on the following attitudes:

Have a desire to do God's will. No — wait. Don't go on to the next one yet. Think about this one. How much of your prayer is really and truly and honestly about discovering God's will? Or is it more about trying to persuade God to follow your will? Hmmm. Can you really hear God's voice clearly if you'll only listen to Him when He says what you want to hear? Do you really mean it when you say, "Thy will be done?"

Be open to God. Completely. As Father Thomas Green, an expert in prayer, puts it, when we're in a relationship with God, we have to be totally open to God, "… a God who is always mysterious and often surprising and disturbing" (*Weeds among the Wheat,* p. 59). Be ready for that.

Nurture your knowledge of God. Contrary to what some around you might like you to believe, God is not anything you want. He's not something to you and something else to the girl at the next locker.

He's not an amorphous, undefined spirit. He's God — the One and Only God, who is Love, Truth, Justice, and Wisdom. If you want to know and recognize God, you have to know who the True God really is, and the only way to do this is to read the Scriptures and participate in the ancient, wise, and experienced prayer of the Church.

> Do we really care about uniting ourselves to the desires of Christ? Are we concerned, first of all, with the thought Christ has for us, for each of "our activities?" Or is our prayer too often just the running of a kind of "interior film," intended just for ourselves? Or else a more or less melancholy, sterile monologue? Or a search for "ideas on" things, instead of being a profound examination of our soul for the purpose of listening to the real desires of Christ's soul and praying "in his name?"
>
> — Bernard Bro, O.P.,
> *The Rediscovery of Prayer*

Good start. Here you are, praying in openness and with a desire to hear whatever it is God has to say. How do you know when He says it?

Remember that the way you're going to sense God's will in your prayer is through your thoughts and, to a lesser and less trustworthy degree, your emotions. (More on that later.)

There are, essentially, two pretty simple rules that should help you in most of your prayer.

First, compare what you're sensing to Scripture. We know and trust that God reveals Himself through the Scripture, so if what you're sensing fits with that, it's probably from God.

(And I mean really, truly, and honestly fits. Not fits if I twist Jesus' words, give them another meaning, rationalize them, or decide that only part of the message applies to me right now.)

So, open that Bible. Listen to those readings at Mass. You want to hear God speak? Start there, then move on to your own heart, then back again. If what you're feeling, for example, is a strong desire to avoid prayer and go out and do lots of bad stuff, chances are, that particular set of feelings isn't from God, even if it makes you feel momentarily "happy." Just remember this: It wouldn't be called "temptation" if it weren't, well, tempting . . . which means it (whatever "it" is at the moment) gives us a temporary feeling of happiness or pleasure.

Secondly, follow this guideline, also from Father Green: "[God] always works in peace, and usually slowly" (*Opening to God,* 51).

In other words, if it's God you're interacting with, you'll be at peace — real, complete, deep peace — not a quick rush of happiness or excitement. It doesn't mean that what you're sensing will immediately please you, either. It may annoy, upset, or anger you. Truth can do that. But once you get over those feelings, you'll feel peace — a sense that whatever is going on, no matter how inconvenient or mysterious, is something good that you could tell the whole world about and not be ashamed of.

So: Be open, be committed to God's will, and make sure your prayer is about who God really is, not about who you'd like God to be. Measure what you're sensing against what God's revealed about Himself in Scripture and Church Tradition. Judge whether the direction you're understanding is bringing you peace or anxiety.

And most of all, look at the fruit of your prayer. Your connection with God is going to be leading you to make choices. Are these choices about God's love? If the answer is yes, stop worrying. You're on the right road. You're listening.

> Then the LORD said, "Go outside and stand on the mountain before the LORD; the LORD will be passing by." A strong and heavy wind was rending the mountains and crushing rocks before the LORD — but the LORD was not in the wind. After the wind there was an earthquake — but the LORD was not in the earthquake.

After the earthquake there was fire — but the LORD *was not in the fire. After the fire there was a tiny whispering sound.*

When he heard this, Elijah hid his face in his cloak and went and stood at the entrance of the cave. A voice said to him, "Elijah, why are you here?" (1 KINGS 19:11-13)

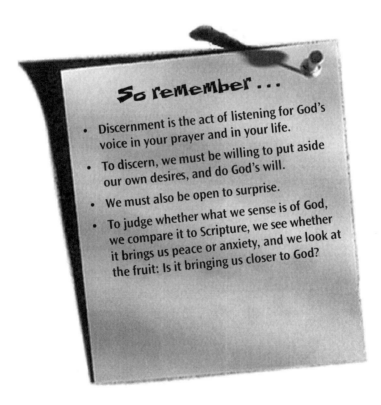

So remember . . .

- Discernment is the act of listening for God's voice in your prayer and in your life.

- To discern, we must be willing to put aside our own desires, and do God's will.

- We must also be open to surprise.

- To judge whether what we sense is of God, we compare it to Scripture, we see whether it brings us peace or anxiety, and we look at the fruit: Is it bringing us closer to God?

PRAYER AND THE REST OF YOUR LIFE

So what is prayer all about, really?

You've learned that prayer isn't a self-help technique or an easy recipe for some superficial sense of happiness. You've learned that prayer isn't about bending God to see your point of view, but more about letting God in your heart so you can see the world as it really, really is, which is from His point of view.

You've learned that there are lots of ways to pray. There are those we've discussed in this book, and lots more — we didn't even touch on using journals and diaries as a form of prayer, or art, or group prayer, or liturgical and ritual prayer. There are, in essence, as many ways to pray as there are people, and the only "right way" to pray is the one that opens your soul to the presence of God.

> In order to profit from this path [of prayer] and ascend to the dwelling places we desire, the important thing is not to think much but to love much; and so, do that which best stirs you to love.
> — Teresa of Ávila, *Interior Castle,* IV, 1.7, 11

You've learned that most of the rational-sounding reasons we have not to pray are really nothing but excuses. We spout all kinds of smart words doubting prayer, but all we're really saying is that we're afraid to pray because we're terrified of what we might hear when we just shut up and listen.

You've learned that the best way to see prayer is as the way we express our friendship with God. When we see our relationship with God as a friendship, and hold ourselves up to the same standards as we would in a good, authentic friendship, we can't go wrong: Take time, listen, be honest, be loving, be humble. It works with friendship, and it's the only way to make your friendship with God real and alive as well.

You've learned that if you want to really learn how to pray, you have to be willing to be taught, and the best place to start is with Jesus. Jesus says to be humble in prayer. He says to come to God as a child or a poor person, deeply aware of our dependence on God. He tells us to accept God's love and forgiveness. He says to pray all the time, and to never, ever stop laying out our requests and our hearts before God.

You've learned that prayer isn't a matter of trying really hard or achieving a goal. It's a matter of relaxing, being committed to God as God is, not as you want Him to be, and letting Him in. You've learned that the desire you're feeling to pray is no less than an invitation from God to turn to Him. You've learned to trust.

> ... A saint isn't somebody who tries harder, but somebody who trusts more.
> — Peter Kreeft, *Prayer*

That should be enough to get you started, I think.

Except for one more, little, tiny point.

This praying, this relationship, is not just about you 'n' God locked up in your room, having nice chats and feeling all chummy.

Praying is about you making so much space for God in your heart that it positively overflows into the rest of your life.

It's about loving God and growing in love for His creation and every one of His children.

It's about listening to God and doing what you discern to be His will in school, at work, in your family, and in every little choice you make during the course of a day.

It is, in the end, about doing what Paul says:

Pray without ceasing. (1 THESSALONIANS 5:17)

You've probably heard that before, and wondered how, exactly, you were supposed to do that. Maybe now you know: Those conscious moments and minutes and prayer will open your heart to God and make room for him, so that eventually, all the time, you're conscious of the amazing truth that God is with you, God loves you, and God loves through you.

> Jesus, hope of the penitent
> How kind You are to those who ask
> How good You are to those who seek
> What must You be to those who find?
> — St. Bernard of Clairvaux

So if you're still worried about prayer, and still worried about whether it's "working" (and please stop trying to think that way, but until you do …), just look at your life and consider:

- Are you loving more?
- Are you more Christ-like in your dealings with others?
- Is your life more closely attuned to the Gospel?
- Are you starting to put more importance on what God thinks than on what others think?
- Are you more attuned to the pain and hurt of others, and more willing to let God work through you to help?
- Are you at peace with yourself? Has your trust in God deepened?

If you can answer "yes" or even "I think so" to these questions, then be assured that your prayer is "working," because it's bringing you into more intimate terms with God.

I hope — no, I pray — that this little book has helped you on that journey. I pray that the words of a great saint that I'm going to end

with will help you, too, that they'll give you the strength and vision to keep praying today, tomorrow, and the rest of your days because you know, at the end of life, there's not a single soul who looks back and says, "Gee, I wish I hadn't prayed so much."

> Do not look forward to what may happen
> tomorrow.
> The same Eternal Father who cares for you
> today
> Will take care of you tomorrow
> And every day of your life.
> He will either shield you from suffering,
> Or He will give you unfailing strength to
> bear it.
> Be at peace, then, and put aside all anxious
> thoughts.
> — St. Francis de Sales

SUGGESTED PRAYERS AND BIBLE PASSAGES

I. Old Prayers, Still New

The Lord's Prayer
Our Father, who art in heaven,
hallowed be thy name;
thy kingdom come;
thy will be done
on earth as it is in heaven.
Give us this day our daily bread;
and forgive us our trespasses
as we forgive those
who trespass against us;
and lead us not into temptation,
but deliver us from evil.
Amen.

The Hail Mary
Hail Mary, full of grace,
The Lord is with thee.
Blessed art thou among women,
And blessed is the fruit of thy womb, Jesus.
Holy Mary, Mother of God,
Pray for us sinners,
now and at the hour of our death.
Amen.

 PRAYER

The Doxology
Glory be to the Father,
and to the Son,
and to the Holy Spirit.
As it was in the beginning,
is now and ever shall be,
world without end.
Amen.

The Apostles' Creed
I believe in God, the Father almighty,
creator of heaven and earth.
I believe in Jesus Christ, his only Son, our Lord.
He was conceived by the power of the Holy Spirit
and born of the Virgin Mary.
He suffered under Pontius Pilate, was crucified, died, and was
   buried.
He descended to the dead.
On the third day he rose again.
He ascended into heaven, and is seated at the right hand of the
   Father.
He will come again to judge the living and the dead.
I believe in the Holy Spirit,
the holy catholic Church,
the communion of saints,
the forgiveness of sins,
the resurrection of the body,
and the life everlasting. Amen.

— *INTERNATIONAL CONSULTATION ON ENGLISH TEXTS*

Act of Contrition

My God, I am sorry for my sins with all my heart. In choosing to do wrong and failing to do good, I have sinned against you whom I should love above all things. I firmly intend, with your help, to do penance, to sin no more, and to avoid whatever leads me to sin. Our Savior Jesus Christ suffered and died for us. In his name, my God, have mercy.

— *THE CATHOLIC SOURCE BOOK, BROWN-ROA (2000), P. 8*

Act of Faith

O my God, I believe that You are one God in three Divine Persons: Father, Son and Holy Spirit. I believe that Your Divine Son became Man and died for our sins, and that He will come to judge the living and the dead. I believe these and all the truths that the Catholic Church teaches, because You have revealed them, who can neither deceive nor be deceived. Amen.

Act of Hope

O my God, relying on Your almighty power and infinite mercy and promises, I hope to obtain pardon of my sins, the help of Your grace and life everlasting through the merits of Jesus Christ, my Lord and Redeemer. Amen.

Act of Love

O my God, I love You above all things with my whole heart and soul, because You are all good and worthy of all my love. I love my neighbor as myself for the love of You. I forgive all who have injured me, and ask pardon of all whom I have injured. Amen.

II. Morning Prayers

Give us, Lord, a humble, quiet, peaceable, patient, tender and charitable mind, and in all our thoughts, words and deeds a taste of the Holy Spirit. Give us, Lord, a lively faith, a firm hope, a fervent char-

ity, a love of you. Take from us all lukewarmness in meditation, dullness in prayer. Give us fervour and delight in thinking of you and your grace, your tender compassion towards me. The things that we pray for, good Lord, give us grace to labour for: through Jesus Christ our Lord, Amen.

— *St. Thomas More*

Through every moment of this day: Be with me Lord.
Through every day of all this week: Be with me Lord.
Through every week of all this year: Be with me, Lord.
Through every year of all this life: Be with me Lord.
So that when time is past,
By grace I may at last,
Be with you, Lord.

Grant, O Lord, that none may love thee less this day because of
    me;
That never word or act of mine may turn one soul from thee;
And ever daring, yet one other grace would I implore,
That many souls this day, because of me, may love thee more.

Take, O Lord, and receive all my liberty, my memory, my understanding, and all my will, all that I have and possess. You have given all of these to me; to you I restore them. All are yours, dispose of them all according to your will. Give me your love and your grace; having but these I am rich enough and ask for nothing more.

— *St. Ignatius of Loyola (Catholic Source Book, p. 34)*

Breathe in me, O Holy Spirit,
That my thoughts may all be hold.
Act in me, O Holy Spirit,
That my work, too, may be holy.

Draw my heart, O Holy Spirit,
That I love but what is holy.
Strengthen me, O Holy Spirit,
To defend all that is holy.
Guard me then, O Holy Spirit,
That I always may be holy.

— *St. Augustine (Catholic Source Book, P. 31)*

III. Evening Prayers

Nunc Dimittis

At last, all powerful master, you give leave to your servant to go in peace, according to your promise. For my eyes have seen your salvation which you have prepared for all nations, the light to enlighten the Gentiles and give glory to Israel, your people. Give praise to the Father almighty, to his son, Jesus Christ, the Lord, to the spirit, who dwells in our hearts, both now and forever.

Save us, O Lord, while waking,
And guard us while sleeping,
That when we wake, we may watch with Christ,
And when we sleep, we may rest in peace. Amen.

— *from the Roman Breviary, Prayer at Compline*

Watch, dear Lord with those who wake or watch or weep tonight, and give your angels charge over those who sleep. Tend your sick ones, O Lord Jesus Christ, rest your weary ones, bless your dying ones, soothe your suffering ones, shield your joyous ones, and all for your love's sake.

—*St. Augustine (Catholic Source Book, P. 31)*

O Lord, our God, what sins I have this day committed in word, deed, or thought, forgive me, for you are gracious, and you love all

men. Grant me peaceful and undisturbed sleep, send me your guardian angel to protect and guard me from every evil, for you are the guardian of our souls and bodies, and to you we ascribe glory, to the Father and the Son and the Holy Spirit, now and for ever and unto the ages of ages.

— *Russian Orthodox Prayer*

IV. Other Good Prayers

Guardian Angel Prayer
O angel of God, my guardian dear,
to whom his love commits me here,
Ever this day, be at my side,
To light and guard, to rule and guide. Amen.

Breastplate of St. Patrick
Christ be with me, Christ within me,
Christ behind me, Christ before me,
Christ beside me, Christ to win me,
Christ to comfort me and restore me,
Christ beneath me, Christ above me,
Christ in quiet, Christ in danger,
Christ in the hearts of all that love me,
Christ in the mouth of friend and stranger.

Anima Christi
Soul of Christ, be my sanctification.
Body of Christ, be my salvation.
Blood of Christ, fill all my veins.
Water of Christ's side, wash out my stains.
Passion of Christ, my comfort be.
O good Jesus, listen to me.
In Thy wounds I fain would hide,

N'er to be parted from Thy side;
Guard me, should the foe assail me.
Call me when my life shall fail me.
Bid me come to Thee above,
With Thy saints to sing Thy love
World without end. Amen.

V. Other Prayers to Mary

Hail, Holy Queen *(Salve Regina)*

Hail, Holy Queen, Mother of Mercy,
our life, our sweetness and our hope.
To thee do we cry, poor banished children of Eve.
To thee do we send up our sighs, mourning and weeping
in this valley of tears.
Turn, then, O most gracious Advocate, thine eyes of mercy
  toward us;
and after this, our exile, show unto us the blessed fruit of thy
  womb, Jesus.
O clement, O loving, O sweet Virgin Mary.

Pray for us, O Holy Mother of God
That we may be made worthy of the promises of Christ.

The Memorare

Remember, O most gracious Virgin Mary, that never was it known that anyone who fled to your protection, implored your help, or sought your intercession was left unaided.

Inspired by this confidence, we fly unto you, O virgin of virgins, our Mother. To you we come, before you we stand, sinful and sorrowful. O Mother of the Word Incarnate, despise not our petitions, but in your mercy hear and answer me. Amen.

Praying with Scripture

These are Scripture passages particularly good for prayer, especially if you're new to prayer. They're only a beginning, though.

Some of these passages are longer, some are short. Break up the longer passages, and pray with a few verses each day. Or, pray with a longer story for several days in a row.

Remember: Read slowly, and let the Lord speak to you. Listen.

When You're Feeling Great and Want to Thank God
Psalm 145
Psalm 139

When You're Feeling Grateful for God's Mercy
Psalm 29
Psalm 144

When You're Feeling Unsure and Anxious
Psalm 23
Philippians 4:4-7
Romans 8:31-39

When You're Seeking God's Forgiveness
Psalm 51
Luke 15
John 8:1-11

When You Need a Reminder That You Belong to Christ
Mark 2:13-17
1 John 4:7-21
Romans 14:8-12

When You're Wondering How You Should Live
Matthew 5-7
Matthew 19:13-30
Mark 8:24-38
Ephesians 5:1-20
Philippians 3:2-16
Philippians 4:8-9
Colossians 3:12-17

When You're Fighting Temptation
Matthew 5:27-48
Ephesians 6:10-17

When You Want to Focus on Jesus
John 1:1-18
John 6:22-59
Philippians 2:5-11
Colossians 1:15-20

The Birth of Jesus
Matthew 1-2
Luke 1-2:40

The Passion (Suffering and Death) of Jesus
Matthew 26-27
Mark 14-15
Luke 22-23
John 18-19

The Resurrection of Jesus
Matthew 28
Mark 16
Luke 24
John 20-21

But I want more!

Like **Prove It! Prayer?** You'll love these other titles in the Prove It! series by Amy Welborn ...

Prove It! God

The first in the series, **Prove It! God** answers the REAL questions you have about God, evolution, good and evil, and a whole lot of other things you never hear about in religion class, in Sunday homilies, or from your parents. You have nothing to lose – but your doubts!

0-87973-396-9, (396) paper, 128 pp.

Prove It! Church

What do you say when someone tells you you're not a Christian because what your church teaches isn't in the Bible, or you worship Mary like a goddess? **Prove It! Church** gives you the answers, proving the Catholic Church belongs to Christ and *is* Christ in the world today.

0-87973-981-9, (981) paper, 160 pp.

Prove It! Jesus

You know Jesus. He died on the cross, right? He preached and healed and worked miracles. But do you *really* know Jesus? Do you know why you believe what you believe, and how to defend it to others? **Prove It! Jesus** provides the fascinating facts for a fuller faith in the Son of God.

0-87973-544-9, (544) paper, 128 pp.

ABOUT THE AUTHOR

Amy Welborn has an M.A. in religion from Vanderbilt University. She taught high school theology for nine years. Since 1994, she has been writing a syndicated column on Catholic youth for Catholic News Service and is a columnist for *Our Sunday Visitor*.

200 Noll Plaza / Huntington, IN 46750
1-800-348-2440 / osvbooks@osv.com / www.osv.com
Availability of books subject to change without notice.   A29BBABP

Are you good to go?

You are with the Catholic Pocket Prayer Book!

Small enough to fit in the teeniest purse, the most overstuffed backpack, or, of course, a pocket ... but big enough to hold the thoughts of your heart.

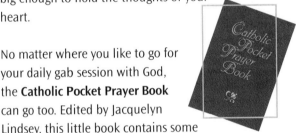

No matter where you like to go for your daily gab session with God, the **Catholic Pocket Prayer Book** can go too. Edited by Jacquelyn Lindsey, this little book contains some of Catholicism's most beloved and beautiful prayers to help kick-start your communication with our Creator, or fill the space when you're at a loss for words.

1-931709-43-2, (T26) leatherette, 272 pp.

Is your family inspired by your prayer life?
Check out the **Catholic Family Prayer Book,** also by Jacquelyn Lindsey.
0-87973-999-1, (999) leather, 384 pp.

Our Sunday Visitor

200 Noll Plaza / Huntington, IN 46750
1-800-348-2440 / osvbooks@osv.com / www.osv.com
Availability of books subject to change without notice.   A29BBABP

Our Sunday Visitor ...

YOUR SOURCE FOR DISCOVERING THE RICHES
OF THE CATHOLIC FAITH

Our Sunday Visitor has an extensive line of materials for young children, teens, and adults. Our books, Bibles, booklets, CD-ROMs, and audio and video products are available in bookstores worldwide.
To receive a FREE full-line catalog or for more information, call Our Sunday Visitor at 1-800-348-2440.
Or write Our Sunday Visitor / 200 Noll Plaza / Huntington, IN 46750.

• •

____ Please send me a catalog.
Please send me materials on:

____ Apologetics and catechetics   ____ Reference works
____ Prayer books   ____ Heritage and the saints
____ The family   ____ The parish

Name: _____

Address: _____ Apt.: _____

City: _____ State: ____ ZIP: ____

Telephone: (___) _____ A29BBABP

• •

____ Please send a friend a catalog.
Please send a friend materials on:

____ Apologetics and catechetics   ____ Reference works
____ Prayer books   ____ Heritage and the saints
____ The family   ____ The parish

Name: _____

Address: _____ Apt.: _____

City: _____ State: ____ ZIP: ____

Telephone: (___) _____ A29BBABP

• •

OurSundayVisitor

200 Noll Plaza / Huntington, IN 46750 / 1-800-348-2440 / osvbooks@osv.com / www.osv.com